Electronic Engine Tuning

Writing engine maps for road and race cars.

by

Cathal Greaney

Sept 2012

ISBN 978-1-291-09470-1

Electronic Engine Tuning
by Cathal Greaney

ISBN 978-1-291-09470-1

Sept 2012 First Edition

Acknowledgements

I would like to thank the many satisfied customers I've had over the past ten years. The customers and enthusiasts I've met while running my Engine Tuning business from 2002 to 2006 and my engine tuning training business from 2006 onwards has given me the insight and experience necessary to write this book.

I would also like to thank my parents for helping me get a great education in electronics and software development and encouraging me as a teenager to experiment on race and rally cars and to explore my interests in racing, rallying and car electronics.

About the Author

Cathal Greaney is a software engineer living in Galway, Ireland. He founded and ran Tightrope Technology Motorsport Ltd from 2002 to 2006. He then specialized in providing training for other motorsport professionals in the engine tuning field.

Cathal has a Bachelor's Degree in Electronic Engineering and a Masters Degree in Computer Systems from the University of Limerick, Ireland.

Cathal can be contacted at:

irishapps@gmail.com

http://www.cathalgreaney.ie

Preface

My aim in writing this book is to provide a straight forward and easy to use guide to the beginner and seasoned mechanic/engine tuner. The book explains the fundamentals of engine tuning in an easy to follow and linear manner. The reader can go chapter by chapter or skip to whichever section interests them.

The book begins with an introduction to Electronic Engine Tuning and covers the tools necessary for electronic tuning, the software required and other basics.
The book then takes an in depth look at Fuel Injection, Ignition, Boost Control and Water Injection from the point of view of the electronic tuner.

There is a dedicated chapter dealing with tuning for different fuel types and octane levels.

Finally, I wrap things up by discussing the fundamentals of 1 dimensional and 2 dimensional mapping and providing a checklist for the beginner tuner to use when setting up an ECU on a new engine.

Table of Contents

Table of Contents

Table of Contents

Table of Contents

Appendix

1. Introduction

Engine tuning has a broad definition and can mean any change to the engines design and operation in order to increase power output, efficiency or other characteristic that the tuner has in mind. We will mention tuning for efficiency and economy at some points throughout this book, but our primary concern will be tuning an engine for maximum power output. We will be discussing different techniques for increasing an engines brake horsepower and torque. We will discuss the different approaches and characteristics required to tune for circuit racing, rallying and drag racing.

Additionally, we will be limiting ourselves to using the electronic components of the engine for tuning. We will not delve too deeply into the mechanical changes required to tune an engine, except for the way in which they affect the electronic tuning of an engine. In other wards, we will assume that all the mechanical changes have been made to the engine and we are then setting up the electronics so that they work with the existing or new mechanical specification.

However, I believe that reading this book will give you an excellent insight into both the mechanical and electronic aspects of tuning a modern performance car.

One more point to make about electronic engine tuning. I have almost never come across a car or engine that I couldn't improve in some way by making adjustments to the electronics. If the engine and electronics are standard then these changes are often dramatic. However, tuning means tuning… if an engine or car happens to already be close to its optimum settings either because it has already been tuned by a professional or because it just happens to be near perfectly tuned, then there isn't much you can do to increase it's performance. Never make changes just for the sake of it. If your testing reveals that the fuel and ignition settings are already at optimal levels then don't adjust them unless you are doing it for training purposes or you are doing it to confirm that the engine is tuned.

1.1 Objectives

After reading this book you will know how to:

1. Take a standard road going engine and increase its performance without making any mechanical changes to it.

2. Take an engine that has been mechanically altered and tuning it to work in its new mechanical configuration.

3. Optimize an engine to give maximum torque OR maximum horsepower based on the users wishes.

4. Know the different characteristics that make for a well tuned road, rally or race car.

5. Tune for maximum performance.

6. Tune for maximum reliability.

7. Tune for maximum fuel efficiency(if you want to).

8. Understand all the fundamentals necessary for professional engine tuning, both mechanical and electronic

1.2 The Basics

- The manufacturer usually makes a lot of compromises when mapping the EMU.
- Most production maps can be adjusted to give more power with better fuel efficiency.
- The engine management system should be updated every time a change is made.
- Even simple induction and exhaust changes should be accompanied by a fuel and ignition map change.

The Engine Management Unit (EMU) controls all the engine systems in a modern car. The two primary systems being controlled are the fuel injection system and the ignition system. Almost all other electrical systems are also controlled directly or indirectly via smaller ECUs by the main EMU.

The EMU uses fuel and ignition maps to control the engine at all loads and RPM levels. The AFR and the ignition advance are controlled in this way.

Key elements in the successful installation and mapping of an EMU are a comprehensive understanding of the engines varying fuel delivery and ignition requirements over a broad range of operating conditions and study of the factors influencing the engine's fuel and spark needs measured and interpreted by the control systems. A thorough understanding of the electronic systems affected by the EMU and of the electronic systems on-board the EMU itself and a good knowledge of software systems is also essential... these latter two areas are the most neglected or lacking in most tuning environments.

Motec

GEMS

Autronic

Emerald

1.3 Basics Concepts

These topics will be discussed in greater detail later, for now here is a brief outline of the basic concepts:

Air-Fuel Ratio

The engine has basic demands for air and fuel. The air-fuel mix can be manipulated to improve driveability, increase economy and horsepower and control the emissions.

The main function of the fuel delivery system is to mix the air and fuel in the correct ratios dictated by the EMU. Small variations in AFR can have a dramatic effect on power and economy.

A rich mixture is one with a lower AFR. There is insufficient oxygen to support complete combustion of the fuel. Rich mixtures increase fuel consumption and emissions of hydrocarbons and carbon monoxide. They tend to reduce power, increase carbon deposits and foul spark plugs and dilute the engine oil.

A lean mixture is the opposite. A larger AFR with more air than is necessary for complete combustion. The fuel will burn more slowly and at a higher combustion temperature. Lean mixtures reduce power, elevate engine temperatures and increase emissions of oxides of nitrogen. It also causes driveability problems and can lead to engine destruction.

Stoichiometric Ratio

This is the ratio of the air to the fuel. Different ratios are suitable for different engines, conditions and applications. For a modern engine the AFR must be controlled very carefully and accurately. The best mixture for the most complete combustion and the best compromise between lean and rich mixtures is often the wrong mixture to use on forced induced and tuned NA engines.

The stoichiometric ratio can also be represented as lambda. One Lambda equals a ratio of 14.7:1 air to fuel.

Mixture Control for Power, Economy, Emissions

Power is always a concern, but so too is the demand for good fuel economy and reduced emissions.

On a perfectly mapped system, adjusting the system for maximum power will mean increasing fuel consumption. Minimizing fuel consumption means sacrificing power and driveability. Both max power and max fuel efficiency means increased emissions.

A good mapper can deliver good power, quick starting and smooth trouble free driving without sacrificed fuel efficiency. Most production maps can be adjusted to give more power with better fuel efficiency.

Ignition Timing

In terms of all four major aspects of performance – power, fuel economy, emissions and driveability – ignition control is equally as important as the air-fuel mix. Combustion in the cylinders takes a certain amount of time. Simultaneous control of the fuel and ignition is essential to engine tuning.

For cold start, the best ignition timing is near TDC(top dead centre). More advanced timing allows the engine to fire while the piston is still rising. If the engine is hot, retarded ignition timing can prevent reverse torque and starter damage. It is desirable to retard ignition timing for low cranking speed conditions and more advanced ignition is permissible under less challenging warm starts.

After starting, the ignition timing can be advanced to improve the engine running and to reduce the requirement for enrichment. After this ignition retard can be used to quickly heat the lambda sensor and cat. Advancing the timing during warm-up under part throttle will improve power and driveability and fuel economy.

Acceleration

Opening the throttle very quickly places demands on the engine. The sudden transition from closed throttle to fully open throttle raises the manifold pressure and additional fuel is required, but this fuel is not instantly available. There is a lag between the ideal and actual delivery of fuel.

For quick smooth throttle responses the basic air and fuel sensing is too slow. The fuel system must be able to compensate for rapid increases in manifold pressure. Acceleration enrichment is used to provide the required throttle response and the tuner must set up the parameters in the EMU to achieve this…. Some basic EMUs do this automatically.

In most systems a separate acceleration enrichment table must be programmed to achieve this and a competition table will be very different to a standard road table.

1.4 Basics of High Performance Mapping

Nearly all mods to the engine to increase power, revolve around improving the volumetric efficiency of the engine so that more air can flow into the cylinders on each stroke. The gains may be tailored to the middle or top end of the power band. Higher lift and longer duration cams, larger valves, ported heads, better intake manifolds and exhaust headers, free flowing exhausts and induction systems all do the same basic job.. improve air flow. And of course forced induction forces more oxygen into the cylinders.
The fuel system must compensate for this increase in air. The standard EMU and fuel and ignition setup is designed to be optimum at the standard air flow and when we increase the air flow we can quickly go outside of the stock EMUs most efficient range of operation and when we go to more extreme states of tune we can go completely outside of the stock EMUs range of operation.

For every modification made to the engine, a remap of the air-fuel and ideally of the ignition is necessary to gain the full value of the changes. A few horsepower may be liberated without remapping, but to get any significant performance increase, a remap is required.

The Stoichiometric mixture setting(or the Lambda setting) on all production cars are not optimized for peak power, so a remap without changing anything else on the car will immediately liberate some power. Peak power is achieved with a slightly richer mixture in some areas of the power band and a leaner mixture in other places. There are some exceptions(such as the Subaru Impreza), but in general, we can achieve more power AND better fuel economy than the production EMU... this is especially true on hot hatches and almost all NA cars(the downside is slightly higher emissions, but still well within the NCT limits). Even cars with very aggressive full throttle tables can be significantly improved.

Conservative fuel control is usually accompanied by conservative ignition mapping... mainly because most manufacturers have to limit themselves to operating on 91octane fuel. The revised fuel control mentioned above can be further enhanced by better ignition mapping, tailored specifically for the fuel you are running on(normally 95 octane).

Trying to adjust the stock EMU without using a replacement or piggyback unit will at the very best produce a purely linear response in fuel and ignition change. You can tune one point in the power curve for best power, but the rest of the power curve will suffer. Resulting in a big drop in overall power. The net result is that even the area you tuned will show less power because the surrounding load sites will be operating at reduced power and the added theoretical power of the site you tuned won't have enough shove to overcome the reduced power of the points immediately before and after this point. We know every trick in the book when it comes to tweaking stock EMUs and the best that can be achieved is a perceived increase in power, but on inspection on the dyno, you end up with a slower car. These tweaks include upping or lowering the fuel pressure, altering the mass air flow sensor or the throttle sensor or the manifold absolute pressure sensor etc... all these changes produce a LINEAR change in air-fuel mix that isn't of real practical value. On the ignition side, you can rotate the crank angle sensor, or modify other sensors such as the ref or trigger sensors and in this way achieve a linear change in ignition advance or retard. The difference here is that you run the risk of detonation and pre-ignition which will lead to head gasket failure is you're lucky and piston meltdown on a worst case scenario.
To repeat, the only way to properly remap is to use a fully mappable replacement EMU or to use a good piggyback EMU.

The exception to this is the boost pressure on turbo and blown cars. Upping the boost a little by altering the waste gate in some way(electronically or mechanically), will normally give a nice power increase across the entire charged power curve – without any change to the EMU. Obviously no gains are available in the off boost area. However, care must be taken to keep within safe limits. Once you go past a certain limit(different on each car) you can say goodbye to your head gasket or at worst suffer complete engine failure. A good example is the Celica GT4. The factory boost level is 0.7bar(depending on year), and on 95 octane the engine will happily run at 0.9bar, but much past this, without any other mods to exhaust or induction is not advisable. Competition engines can run at 1.3bar on 97 octane, but a revised head gasket is advised.
Note: just changing the induction and exhaust will usually up the boost without going near the waste gate or the EMU(e.g. Skyline GTR). Always monitor the boost levels after every change to the engine, even if the change isn't intended to modify the boost level.

Also note, just because the engine appears to run OK after a boost change doesn't mean that you aren't doing permanent long-term damage. Any change should be carried out on the dyno with all the diagnostic and knock – detonation sensors attached. The engine should then be run at full power for a sustained period and all parameters carefully monitored.

2. Tools for Advanced Tuning

2.1 Computer

The computer is the most important tool for tuning an ECU. In most cases you can't do ANY tuning without a computer to interface with the ECU. Exceptions are ECUs that are shipped with small interface boxes like the Link and Apexi ECUs. However, it is often quicker to disregard the control boxes and use a computer to program these ECUs.

Fortunately, you don't need a particularly powerful PC. The PC itself doesn't need to do much processing. It is primarily used simply as an interface. Therefore, any old PC will normally do the trick. However, there are some basic requirements.

Naturally, your computer must have the correct port for interfacing with the ECU. If your ECU requires a serial interface then the computer must have a 9pin serial RS232 port. If the ECU requires parallel communications(rare) then your PC must have a 25pin parallel port(i.e. printer port). If your ECU uses a USB or PCMCIA interface then the computer must have these also.

  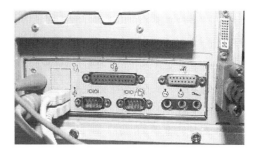

If you are using a computer made before 2002 then you can be pretty sure that it will have the necessary 9pin and 25pin ports. However, it may not have the necessary USB or PCMCIA ports. If your PC is of a newer design 2003 onwards, then it will likely have a USB port and may or may not have a PCMCIA port and it will likely be missing the 9pin or the 25pin connection. If this is the case then you can usually get a converter to go from USB to 9pin serial or to 25pin parallel.
You can also get a USP to PCMCIA adaptor.

Although, your computer doesn't need much processing power to program the ECU, it may need to run a particular operating system to fit in with the needs of the ECU software. Therefore, make sure that your PC can run whatever operating system is required by the ECU software.
For example, if your ECU software is designed to run on Windows XP, then you will need a PC made after 2002 even though you won't be using much of its hardware resources to program the ECU.

Similarly, if your ECU software is designed to work on MS-DOS, then you may need an older computer that has Windows 3.1 or MS-DOS itself installed on it. Some MS-DOS software that interfaces through the serial port won't work well using Windows XP to MS-DOS emulation.

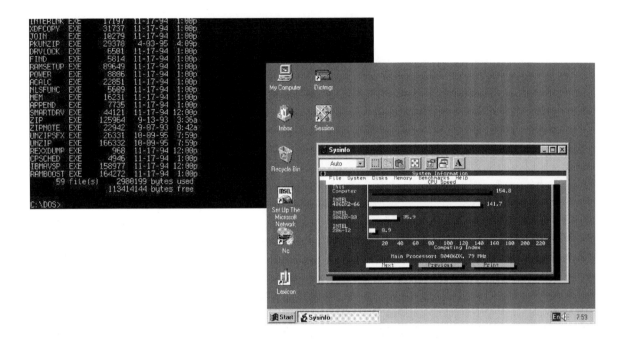

With the rise in open source software available for the engine tuner, there are more and more tuning systems that require the Linux operating system.
Linux is becoming more mainstream and the engine tuner will eventually have to have a Linux based computer to access this software. The good news is that Linux software is usually free.

I would recommend a beginner to use Ubuntu Linux.

2.2 Software

Of course, you will have to use the appropriate software in order to communicate with the ECU. Most ECUs will ship with the required dongles and software. Even if the ECU uses open communications through the serial port, you will still need the proprietary manufacturers software to work with the native hardware of the ECU manufacturer.
Almost all software required these days is free to download from the manufacturers or suppliers website.

Other software that's handy to have are Microsoft Excel or Microsoft Works spread sheet applications.
A decent graphics application to allow screen grabbing and printing.

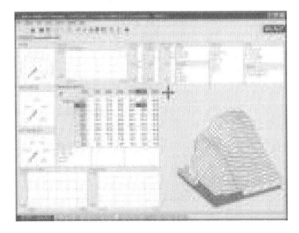
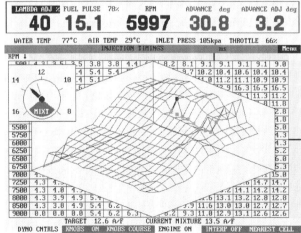

2.3 Communicating with the ECU

CAN Communications

The CAN Communications system is a high speed network communications system that allows multiple devices to be connected and communicate with each other.
The CAN connection is used for all communications with the PC via the ECU Manager software which includes, calibration, diagnostics checking, retrieving the logged data, firmware upgrading and enabling options.

RS232 Serial Communications

Older style input/output communication cable. Still widely used.

Proprietary Communications

A lot of the smaller manufacturers still use their own proprietary communications protocols for editing the ECU information.

- Autronic use a small two pin connector that plugs directly into the ECU board.
- Older Motec OEM use a similar system.
- Hondata use a USB interface.
- Gems/AEM/Omex use serial communications protocols.
- HKS use Cat5 connection cables.
- Apexi use standard RS232 connections.

2.4 Other Equipment

Timing Light

Timing lights are essential to check crank or cam trigger positions. You need to verify that the computer is reading the correct advance angle from the crank position sensor.

A good timing light will allow the strobe to trigger from a high voltage source like a plug wire and from a low voltage source like a direct coil wire.

The dial back facility will allow you to set the Cam timing and to measure other parameters that require dial back e.g.. setting the timing at higher RPM settings.

Compression and Leak Down Tools

Use these tools to check the condition of the combustion chamber. Simply used to confirm tight and even compression in all cylinders. If will highlight worn rings and slightly bent or damaged valves that won't cause a knocking sound.

Multi Meter

Use these tools to check the condition of the combustion chamber. Simply used to confirm tight and even compression

 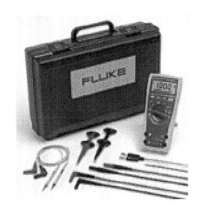

Oscilloscope

SEE APPENDIX C – Diagnostics Testing using the Oscilloscope.
A vital tool for checking a multitude of signals from the sensors and actuators. Particular good for checking the Ref and Sync signals coming from the ECU.

Dyno

Obviously, a vital tool in tuning the engine.
With a dyno you have your car stationary in the workshop and you can operate the engine at full capacity for an extended period of time while observing the power increase/decrease due to your modifications to the ECU.

The less experienced the engine tuner, the more vital it is to have the use of an accurate dyno.

Electronic Stethoscope

Good for pinpointing noise and locating loose bearings and valve noise. It will also highlight dirty injectors, vacuum leaks etc.. Anything sound related under the engine bay. It works in the 50 to 150bB area

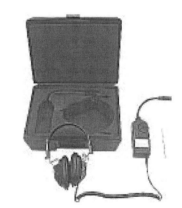

Fuel Pressure Gauge

Another must have for any tuner even if you aren't tuning the ECU.
Fuel pressure is vital during tuning. You must have a good fuel rail reading when tuning. Otherwise you can chase after problems for hours before realising that they are fuel related. The gauge kit must have all of the most common fittings for the main manufacturers. This will save you from having to sever fuel lines and reconnect them after tuning is complete.
If you are tuning a car that you expect to have to look at several times a year then its better to fit a fuel pressure sensor at the fuel rail and send the signal directly back to the ECU and use the PC to view and log fuel pressure. The extra expense of the fuel pressure sensor will be offset by the time saved in connecting and disconnecting the fuel pressure gauge.

Injector Tester

An injector tester(not a flow bench) is a good tool to have to ensure that the injectors are opening and closing. Just because they are clicking doesn't mean that they are opening and closing correctly.

A flow bench is good to use when matching up injectors. However, they are often too expensive to own so its best to bring a bag of injectors with you to a facility that has a flow bench and spend a few hours checking and mating up sets of injectors.

Other Heat and Pressure Gauges

Of course the following inputs are essential when tuning:

- coolant temperature sensor – minimum of one placed in the main coolant flow.
- oil pressure sensor
- oil temperature sensor – ideally three placed at the lower/middle and upper areas of the oil circuit
- air temperature sensor – minimum of one sensor placed close to the MAF sensor.
- charge air temp sensor – ideally one before and one after the intercooler
- boost gauge – closer to the inlet tract the better

Lambda Sensor

We will discuss the importance of this sensor later on, but for now remember the following....

An AFR meter using a one to four wire sensor is no good for wideband tuning. The output of these sensors are binary and can only approximate the air fuel mix. Most of them will only tell you if the engine is running above or below stoic and wont indicate haw far above or below stoic you are. These narrow-band sensors are very sensitive around lambda of 1 but get less and less sensitive the richer you get.

The best sensors to use are the Bosch or NGK five wire sensors. These sensors require interface units to read the correct mixture and won't work by connecting them to a multi meter, but the added expense is well worth it.

3. Fuel Injection

There are many similarities between the older carburettor systems and the current EFI systems. The same rules apply to both the old and current systems.
A large diameter manifold runner will kill low RPM torque while increasing top end BHP whether you are using carbs or injectors.
Increasing carb throttle plate size and the throttle bores will increase high RPM air flow and maximum power at the expense of a fall in mid range output. The same thing will happen on an EFI system is we replace a throttle body and plate with a larger diameter body and plate.
Finely atomised fuel droplets from a carb system that are evenly distributed throughout the intake air charge burn more uniformly and produce more power in the same way as an EFI system.

The major difference between an old carb system and an EFI system is in regard to fuel metering.
With an EFI system, the ECU calculated how long it will open the fuel injectors nozzles to deliver the correct quantity of fuel into the air intake air stream.
The correct length of time that the injectors must spray(pulse width) is determined during dyno testing. If the engine makes 300bhp at 8000rpm with the injectors open for 8.5mS and makes 305bhp with a pulse width of 9mS then the ECU is programmed to give that amount of fuel. This process is repeated across the entire rev and load range.

When car manufacturers start such a process is usually takes over 12 months to generate a full fuel map for the engine. They must map for engine performance, driveability, economy, and government emissions. Competition engines however, can be mapped within a few days.

Before the ECU can determine the correct pulse width it must first be provided with information about the state of the engine and in particular how much air is being consumed by the engine.
Each system used must be looked at and understood, because there are all in widespread use.

3.1 Air Flow Meters

Vane Air Flow Meter
The earliest air flow meters used were vane type meters. A passage is blocked by a spring loaded flap and the air-flow blows the flap open to a certain angular position. Connected to the flap pivot is a variable resistor or potentiometer which changes the ECUs input voltage according to how wide the flap has been swung open.
Because air density changes with the ambient temperature as well as other factors, an air-flow meter also houses an air temperature sensor. The air flow meter also has a bypass passage with a mixture adjust screw which allows some air to bypass the sensor flap. This allows the mixture to be tweaked at idle.

MAF – Mass Air Flow Meter

The mass air flow meter or HOT WIRE air flow meter is usually referred to as a MAF sensor(NOT A MAP SENSOR).

It is a tube in the inlet duct through which the air flows to the engine. Within this tube there is a very fine platinum wire, which is heated by an electric current to maintain a constant temperature above ambient. An air temperature sensor beside the MAF sensor signals the ambient temperature to the ECU so that is knows what current to send out to the MAF sensor to keep it at the required temperature. Air passing through the tube cools the wire in direct proportion to the volume of air passing through. The ECU must increase the current in order to keep the wire at the required temperature. It reads this current level as the mass air flow.

Vortex Flow Sensor

The third type of air flow meter is the vortex flow sensor. This uses ultrasonic senders and receivers to measure the rate at which vortices pass through a passage. The signal is read by the ECU and altered for air temperature and barometric pressure and the mass air flow is calculated.

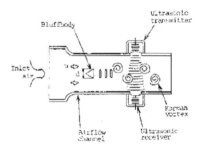

The advantages of the mass air flows systems are that they are very accurate when air flow into the engine varies over a very wide range. They can compensate for slight differences in engine wear and variable specifications.

The major drawbacks of using any of these Mass Air Flow systems from a performance perspective is that they restrict the air flow to a certain extent. The vane type being the major culprit.

Another big performance problem with air flow meters is that inaccurate readings can result due to reverse pulsing in the inlet tract because of long-duration, high-overlap cams.

Speed Density System

To get over the disadvantages of the mass air flow systems, manufacturers developed the speed density system. There is no air-flow meter. Instead, the ECU uses manifold pressure and engine RPM as the major contributors. The ECU also uses info from the charge air temperature and the barometric pressure sensor.

There is no air flow meter to cause restrictions and the manifold pressure sensor will respond to both positive and negative manifold pressure.

These systems are very suitable for turbo and supercharger applications.

Again wild camshafts will cause strong reversion pulses in the inlet tract and give rise to metering difficulties.

AlphaN System

The alphaN system was developed for competition engines only.

The primary inputs come from the throttle position sensor and the crank RPM signal. Again there is no air flow restriction. And the system is immune to reversion problems. However it carries its own quirks and problems. Obviously, accurate throttle input signal is essential to the success of this system. Ease of driving cannot be accurately calculated using this system because there is not enough resolution during the first 5degrees of motion.

3.2 Other Important Inputs

Apart from air flow related inputs, there are several other inputs which are essential to allow the ECU to meter the correct fuel.

When the engine is cold, more fuel must be delivered to ensure it will run and not stutter on acceleration. Based on coolant temperature sensor readings, the ECU will alter the fuel metering until normal operating temperatures are reached.

- Modern competition engines must run much closer to optimum power in order to remain competitive. The dividing line between optimum power and engine destruction is much closer today then even ten years ago. It is no longer possible to maintain a safe rich margin of fuel tuning. Therefore, more inputs are necessary to maintain a closer lean fuel mixture.
- There are fewer fuel molecules in 1cc of hot petrol than in the same volume of cold fuel. Therefore, the true fuel/air mixture will become more lean and send the engine into detonation if the ECU does not adjust the injector pulse width as fuel temperature increases. Of course the opposite is also true. A drop in temperature will cause the mixture to go rich and result in a drop in power. A fuel temperature sensor is required to allow the building of a suitable fuel temperature compensation table.
- Reduced fuel pressure is another problem that must be addressed. Medium pressure drops are not a problem for road going cars because the injection system is designed to maintain regular pressure in the event of falling pressure. However, in competition engines with much higher fuel pressure, small fluctuations in fuel pressure must be compensated for by using a fuel pressure sensor and a suitable ECU compensation table. I you map the engine at 60psi fuel pressure and the battery voltage drops off you could lose the engine because of dropped motor speed and dropped fuel pressure. Blocked fuel filters and partly seized pump bearings have the same effect.

Lambda

The O2 or lambda sensor was originally developed to allow manufacturers to maintain closer control of emissions to comply with exhaust gas regulations. It is fitted to the exhaust downpipe and is a metal coated, ceramic probe that functions like a weak battery, producing about 100mV when oxygen in the exhaust gas is high.

The lambda probe has a different use during tuning or during race conditions. The probe is used to override the ECU outputs when the engine is approaching a dangerously lean condition. You can key in a safe mixture if 14:1 and set the ECU to increase fuel when the mixture goes leaner then this.

Exhaust Gas Temperature

Another vital input in maximum output engines is exhaust gas temperature. EGTs must be kept within safe limits. In some engines a safe limit might be 800degC, but in another engine, a temperature of 70degC can cause the loss of the valve seats.

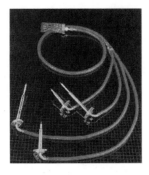

3.3 Inlet Manifolds

Fuel injection systems are defined by the kinds of inlet manifolds used. Different tuning approaches must be adopted depending on the type used.

In multi-point injection where there is at least one injector per cylinder there are two common types of manifold....

The Plenum type and the isolated runner throttle body type.

Plenum Type

Most multi-point systems are plenum type OEM systems. It is often referred to as TPI – Tuned Port injection.

The long manifold runners that join the inlet port and the plenum are of a tuned length to take advantage of the pressure pulses generated in the inlet tract to pump up mid range power and torque. The plenum has a volume about 80% of the engine size and all the manifold runners draw off air from the plenum to the cylinders. Air flow into the plenum is controlled by a throttle body containing either one or two throttle plates.

This system works well in production cars where low and mid range torque is required. However, as power levels rise the long manifold runners begin to restrict air flow and kill top end power.

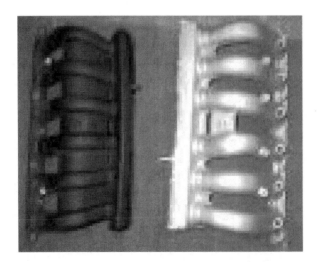

Isolated Runner Type

Plenum types are good at flowing air at low and mid ranges, however, its not all about air flow on the inlet side...

Fuel atomisation and distribution must also be considered. Isolated runners offer a good deal more freedom and allow the tuner to bring the engine closer to the limit of its bhp producing capabilities while still maintaining engine reliability.

When the engine is hot, the air and fuel droplets draw heat from the inlet tract, the cylinder walls, the piston crown, the combustion chamber, the valves and the spark plug. This serves to improve fuel atomisation and therefore enrich the mixture causing waste of fuel and power.

With isolated runners the injectors can be moved further away from the engine. If we use a sequential system, we can mount them outboard of the throttle plates.

Injectors mounted very close to the engine and spraying right at the back of the hot inlet valve improves atomisation, stopping the fuel dropping out of suspension and not burning at low rpm when air speed in the inlet tract is slow. Also, inboard injectors improve low speed and mid range rpm throttle response. In batch fire systems they stop charge robbing.

But in competition engines, we don't have these considerations. We can move the injectors right out to the intake trumpets. From here some of the fuel droplets will smash into the partially open throttle plate and be broken down in size. Other droplets will absorb heat along their journey to the combustion chamber further aiding atomisation. Introducing the fuel so far away from the chamber gives it much more opportunity to evenly mix with the air as it swirls around the throttle plate and down the inlet tract. With improved atomisation and fuel homogenisation we gain some additional power. The improved combustion control allows us to run higher compression or leaner mixtures.

Another way that the isolated runner manifold can improve BHP is by orienting it differently, by turning it upside down, or slightly increasing one runner over another, we can alter the flow and swirl characteristics to improve efficiency and gain another few BHP.

3.4 Fuel Injectors

Dual Injector Setup

Another big advantage of the isolated runner is that we can use two small injectors in each runner instead of using one big injector. Small injectors spraying for longer periods offer better atomisation and finer control over the equivalent larger injector. Long duration dyno sessions are required to determine the duration, location and staging of the two injectors.

In rally cars its preferable to mount one injector inboard close to the stock location and stage it to spray at low rpm. The other injector can be mounted outboard or the throttle plate and can be staged to start spraying at the middle to upper level of the power band... e.g. when the throttle plates are open beyond 50deg.

A race type engine may work better with both injectors outboard of the throttle plate. The intake trumpet injector could be staged to fire first and the other injector could be mounted on the in-box firing directly down the trumpet into the inlet tract. The second injector would be staged to begin firing at maximum torque and when the throttle plate is open beyond 50deg.

 It is also important to remember that bigger bore inlet tracts are not always preferable. You must match your engine configuration with the inlet tract diameter. Smaller diameter manifold tracts serve to improve cylinder filling at engine speeds lower in the power band. They also tend to minimise the intensity of reversion pulsing so there is less restriction at certain RPMs. The other benefit of smaller inlet tracts is that there is greater vacuum which results in improved fuel vaporisation. However, go too small and you will kill top end power.

Timing of the Injector Spray

- **Batch Fire** – all injectors spray simultaneously once every revolution of the crankshaft. Each injector sprays twice during each complete engine cycle. In a 4-cyl engine the firing of the spark plug for cylinders one and four triggers the ECU to commence the spray period for all the injectors... this is why its called a batch fire system. This results in some injectors firing when the inlet valve is closed. Its advantage is that it's a very simple system. The fact that they pulse twice means that the injectors can be much smaller. Also, at lower engine loads the injector spray period can be made longer by programming the ECU to skip every second firing. This improves metering precision when the pulse width is reduced below 2mS.

- **Sequential Fire** – injectors are synchronised to fire with the opening of the inlet valves. In production vehicles it is usual to time the injectors to start firing about 40deg before the inlet valves start to open. Manufacturers use the smallest possible injectors so that at cruise RPM and light engine loads the injectors will finish spraying before the inlet valve closes. This lowers emissions, reduces fuel consumption and improves throttle response. At higher RPM and load, the small injectors pulse width is extended to allow the needed fuel to enter the chambers. The injectors continue to spray fuel long after the inlet valve has closed, and this fuel is then inducted during the next engine cycle... so at higher loads, production sequential injection operates very similar to the batch fire system. This is why there is very little performance gain on production vehicles with sequential injection.

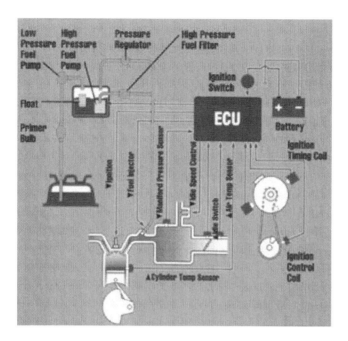

In competition engines we don't have to worry as much about low power performance and exhaust emissions. We can use very large injectors that can supply the engines needs while maintaining a relatively low pulse width. With competition sequential injection the injectors are programmed to stop flowing when the inlet valve has just closed. At lower engine speeds the injectors only start firing mid stroke of the inlet cycle. As RPM and load increase the injectors commence earlier and earlier but still close just as the inlet valve closes. The consensus amongst most competition tuners is that the injectors maximum time open should remain within the opening and closing time of the inlet valve. If the cam has an inlet lobe duration of 300deg the injector pulse width(its spray period) would be limited to 310deg of the crankshaft rotation. However, as we approach max engine speed we usually find a power advantage when the injectors are open for 420deg to 500deg. So if we are using 300deg cams the injectors would open 120deg or more, before the inlet valve opens and finish spraying just before the valve closes.

With a powerful ECU and twin injectors, we can experiment with several configurations to achieve the best power and torque settings.

- the inbound injector can be fixed to fire at 40deg ahead of the inlet valve opening then allow the ECU to determine when injection should cease. The outbound injectors can be set to start firing when the inbound injectors reach a certain pulse width(not always the max pulse width).

Individual cylinder trim is another big advantage of sequential competition setup. Each cylinder is treated as an individual unit and tuned accordingly. The trim from cylinder to cylinder will normally be a max of about 2%.

3.5 Fuel Pressure

The fuel pressure should never be maintained lower than 2.0 bar because lower pressure will cause poor fuel atomisation.

If we are using big injectors, there is often a temptation to use low fuel pressure at low engine speeds, so that the injector duty cycle can be maintained above 50%.

Fuel pressure regulators are required to keep the fuel pressure within a tight margin.
- **Manifold Pressure Reference Regulator.** They increase the dynamic flow range of the fuel injectors. At lower RPM when vacuum levels are high, it allows us to use longer injection pulses which improve atomisation. In turbo engines this regulator allows smaller injectors to be used.
- **Non-Referenced Fixed Pressure Regulator.** Doesn't reference the manifold pressure. Only suitable for naturally aspirated motors – cheap option
- **Non-Referenced Adjustable Pressure Regulator.** Very suitable for naturally aspirated competition engines…. Handy for quick fuel adjustments on the fly.

3.6 Fuel Pumps

Choose a suitable fuel pump that can supply enough fuel at maximum load and maximum RPM. High pressure roller type fuel pumps are most common.

The pump must be able to supply about 10% more fuel than is required by the engine. However, too big a pump is undesirable because we don't want excess fuel flowing back to the tank and causing the fuel to heat up and thus cause a loss in power.

3.6 Fuel Pumps

4. Ignition

4.1 Ignition Advance
*   Variable ignition advance across the load and RPM range is essential.
*   Ignition mapping is just as important as fuel mapping.

There are many factors which must be considered when deciding how late into the compression stroke we initiate the spark in the cylinder. Most engines give max horsepower when we fire the spark so that max cylinder pressure is reached at 12 to 14deg after top dead centre. To achieve this we must initiate ignition sometime before top dead centre. This is called the ignition advance angle. At low engine speeds it will be around 10deg before TDC and at higher speeds it will be at around 20deg before TDC and higher still it could be 40 to 50deg before TDC.
There variable advance angles are required to give the mixture enough time to burn thoroughly and thus give the max horsepower.
Mixture density, air/fuel ratio and fuel quality all influence the ignition advance angle.
Mixture density itself is influenced by a large number of factors and for lower densities we must start the spark earlier to allow enough time for the low oxygen mix to burn.
Very lean and very rich mixtures also burn slowly and require more spark advance. Ideal mix (13:1) burns quickest and requires less advance.
When efficient exhausts are used, the unscavenged exhaust gas in the cylinders is reduced so that there is more fresh mix to burn so advance angle need to be reduced. This also causes less exhaust molecules to interfere with the mix which further reduced the spark advance angle.
The fuel used also affects advance angle. Petrol burns rapidly so requires less time than other fuels. Alcohol is slower to burn and nitro is even slower. But when an accelerator chemical is added to these fuels, spark advance needs to be reduced.
During dyno setup, an ignition map is built up carefully via the laptop at all engines speeds, boost pressures and throttle openings. Compensating factors are also built in such as inlet charge temperatures, engine coolant temperatures and exhaust turbine temperatures.

4.2 Different Ignition Configurations

Points Type Ignition
*   Old carb system.
*   Outdated since introduction of electronic control.

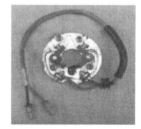

Before electronic ignition became the standard, engines relied on crude points type distributors to time and distribute the spark. One or two coils provided the high voltage spark.
The distributor had two switches, the rotors and the contact breakers and an ignition advance/retard mechanism to vary timing. The switching of the primary circuit was done by the contact breakers (controlled by the distributor cam). When the points were closed, current flowed through the coil, then through the points to earth. This produced a magnetic field surrounding the secondary winding. When the primary magnetic field collapsed (points opened), a current was induced in the secondary winding creating a high voltage current capable of jumping across the spark plug gap.
This high voltage signal flowed from the coil to the rotor then onto the distributor points and onto the sparkplugs.
There are many disadvantages to this setup when tuning an engine and it is impossible to tune an engine in one area without suffering greatly in another. If you tune for top end power and advance etc.... then lower end characteristics suffer etc.... there are lots of ways to combat this by using weights and so on but they only succeed up to a certain point. Once you go beyond 6cyl the situation gets worse.
This system worked well when there was no alternative.

High Energy Ignition
- One of the first electronic ignition systems.
- Adequate for most road applications.
- Not optimum for performance engines.

The common electronic transistor ignition system also uses a contact breaker system and is also on inductive storage type ignition system. It relies on magnetic pulses to open and close the low voltage circuit. The distributor shaft turns a pulse generator rotor inside a permanent magnet. This induces a signal in the pick-up coil. The electric signal flows through the electronic module and switches on and off. Current flows through the primary coil when its on and when its off the magnetic field collapses and just like the old points system, the high voltage signal flows through the distributor to the spark plugs. This system doesn't require tungsten points so a higher current is delivered to the sparkplugs.

 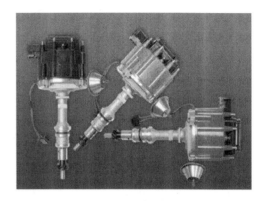

Multi Coil and Capacitor Discharge Ignition
- The only choice for modern performance engines.
- High energy spark and long duration.

But for higher engine speeds and higher intensity spark or longer duration, multi coil or CD Ignition is used. We can opt for a multi coil HEI system or a capacitor discharge system with single or multiple coils.
With multi coils more time is available to saturate each coil fully. But to save money or if the regulations don't allow it, we can use a single coil.
CD ignition stores the ignition energy in a capacitor. Even the best transistor ignition amplifier and coil combination begin to falter at 7500rpm on a v8. even when these rpm speeds are not reached, the CD system is inherently superior to the transistor HEI method and should therefore be used on competition to fast road cars. The bigger, longer duration spark produced by CD systems will always equal or out perform the HEI based systems.
CD ignition in single coil setups wont run out of ignition energy until 10000rpm levels are reached because a capacitor charges and discharges much faster than a coil.
In CD systems, current in the primary circuit powers a mini-oscillator/transformer which charges a capacitor to 400volts. The distributor has a magnetic or LED trigger switch. The amplified signal breaks the primary circuit and the capacitor instantly dumps its energy in the coils primary winding, which steps up the voltage to 30-40000volts which is directed by a rotor button to the sparkplugs.
Conventional HEI systems have a rise time of 100 microsecs; CD has a rise time of 20microseconds. This allows the system to fire fouled and wet plugs which means the car will quickly restart after a stall or a spin.

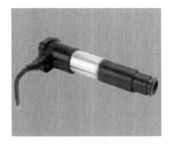   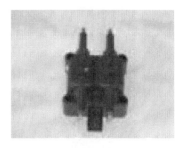

Multi Spark CD Ignition
* Much longer duration spark for sustained burn.
* As much as six sparks per sequence at low revs.

The standard CD ignition produces a spark of short duration. In extreme conditions, turbulence within the chamber might blow out the spark before it gets sufficient heat into the mixture is initiate combustion. This is where multi-spark CD ignition comes in.

This system will give as much as six sparks per spark sequence at idle and will revert to one long duration, high intensity spark at higher rpms and loads.

4.3 Ignition Voltage Requirements

An engines voltage requirements depend on the cylinder pressure and the width of the spark plug gap. An engine running 0.028in gap with a compression ratio of 11:1 will require 20kv to get a spark. At 0.04in and 12.5:1 we require 27kv and at 0.06in and 15:1 we require a minimum of 35kv. In the above three example the stored energy required just to get a spark going will be 10mj, 18mj and 31mj respectively.

Therefore, if our ignition system had a max of 20mj across the spark plug gap, we would have to run with narrow gaps just to get a spark in the 35kv situation. In the 27kv situation we would get a spark but only have 2mj left over to keep the spark gap ionized and get the flame started. But in the 20kv situation we would have enough ignition energy to get the spark going and have a duration long enough to initiate combustion.

So the more secondary ignition energy we have left the better our chances of starting and sustaining combustion at high engine speeds. Also, note that as the compression ratio and plug gap increases, more energy is required to initiate and sustain combustion.

If upgrading the ignition system is not an option because of budgetary constraints or regulations, the opposite must be done, the plug gaps must be reduced to the minimum and the compression ratio must be lowered.

4.4 Choosing an Ignition System

* Most modern stock systems are good.
* When exceeding the factory RPM or using methanol then upgrade.

Modern ignition systems have to operate reliable without misfiring in order to pass government regulations, therefore, the ignition system on most new cars are quite good and will usually be adequate for a stage one or two upgrade. The main area where standard systems have a problem is at very high rpm. Once you go past the max rpm of your stock engine or if you use methanol or alcohol based fuels then you will probably have to upgrade your ignition system.

Another area to consider is reliability. Most stock systems are quite reliable, but there are a few notable exceptions and these systems should be replaced as soon as any mods are undertaken.

4.5 Fitting Ignition Systems

Excessive heat, vibration and moisture must be kept at bay around the ignition system. Mount the spark amplifiers and coil away from the header and turbo and shield them from all local heat sources. Direct a small airflow over the spark box if possible. When fitting components to heat sinks make sure you use heat sink grease. Mount all electronics on anti shock rubber mounts.

Pressurized water jets must never be directed at the ignition system. A tiny amount of water will cause a high-voltage flashover.

Never disconnect any wires with the engine running. Never crank the engine while the leads are disconnected or while the coil lead is disconnected, without first isolating the ignition system. Disconnect the low voltage positive ignition wire at the coil and then you can crank in safety.

Battery chargers and welders operated with the battery connected will also more than likely damage or destroy the ignition system. The main harness going to the spark box as well as any earth straps going to it should also be disconnected when welding. Also place the welder earth close to the welding point.

4.6 Improving Spark Timing Accuracy

• Distributor less systems have best accuracy,

Improved spark timing accuracy can be had by switching to a distributor less system. Harmonics in the valve train can play havoc with the distributor which makes highly accurate spark timing impossible. What should be a 32deg before TDC firing angle at 8000rpm can become a 35deg angle on cylinder one, a 29deg angle on cylinder two, a 33deg angle on cylinder three and a 32deg angle on cylinder four. Because the number one cylinder is firing 3deg advance owing to camshaft spring, we have to retard the timing on all of the other cylinders, just to avoid detonation at number one cylinder. This costs us power. Also, the remaining cylinders are overly retarded and will suffer after burn. This could reduce a turbos life and limit our boost pressure.

When we discard the distributor, we have the option of individual cylinder trim. We can adjust the firing angle to suit each individual cylinder.

Because of engine breathing characteristics, irregular coolant flow (due to head design), fuel and nitrous distribution problems, one cylinder may run hotter or cooler than the others. With ignition trim, we can move power from one cylinder into another.

Without the distributor, another means of informing the EMU when each piston hits TDC must be employed. Rather than using a pulse trigger, we use firing pins embedded in the flywheel. As each pin passes the magnetic pick up sensor a pulse is delivered to the EMU. The EMU then calculated the appropriate advance angle and switched the ignition primary circuit on and off.

On aftermarket systems you need to make sure the pins are placed accurately and that the air gap to the sensor is correct. If firing pin diameters should be the same as the diameter of the sensor pickup. The air gap should be around 0.04in.

4.7 Determining Optimum Ignition Timing

• Least amount of advance for max power.
• Must be mapped on the dyno.

Naturally the ignition timing must be set perfectly for your engine. The least amount of advance required for max power should be used.

The only way to get the timing right is on the dyno. The advance angle should be increased until max torque is reached or until you are beginning to approach detonation. The engine should never actually detonate. A steady state dyno needs to be used to allow proper heat to be loaded into the cylinders otherwise the angle will be overly advanced. Acceleration runs are good for initial setup, but for fine tuning the load must be held at each of the load points.

With turbos, an additional factor must be considered; the spool up of the turbine may be improved by slightly retarding the spark.

If you tune the engine very close to the detonation limit, you must compensate for changes in atmospheric conditions. A 10% increase in relative air density may overlean the mixture and cause piston meltdown, if you don't richen the mixture accordingly. A decrease in humidity might cause engine detonation unless spark advance or the amount of cam advance is reduced.

4.8 Identifying Engine Wreckers

•   Pre-ignition is the main cause of engine failure.

Pre-ignition is caused by extreme combustion temperatures melting the top of the piston and the ring lands. If there is a hole in the piston crown like a welding hole or the centre electrode of the sparkplug is melted then pre-ignition has occurred.
It can usually be traced to combustion chamber or exhaust valve deposits becoming incandescent, bit it may also be caused by blocked water jackets creating a hot spot or a glowing sparkplug with a heat range too hot for the engine. It can also be caused by a hot piston due to lack of lubrication, improper clearance or a broken ring.

•   Excessive cylinder temperatures cause detonation and pre-ignition.
•   Maximum power and economy is achieved just prior to detonation.
•   Detonation is uncontrolled combustion after the spark plug has fired.
•   Pre-ignition is uncontrolled combustion before the spark plug has fired.

Most engines perform best when cylinder pressure peaks at 12-14deg after TDC and performance is usually acceptable with a pressure peak as late as 18-20deg after TDC. Piston acceleration away from TDC is relatively slow, so at the time when combustion pressure is peaking, the combustion space is not rapidly increasing in volume. Because of this, pressure holds at a high level and gives the crankshaft a good shove, making high power.

However, when the charge temp is excessive, detonation occurs and a violent explosion occurs instead of a steady, progressive burn. Obviously this can lead to engine destruction and spark retard is often used to protect against this.
But spark retard in itself can cause engine destruction so a good understanding of detonation and spark retard is essential for any engine tuner.
The positive effects of spark retard as follows...
The fuel burn is started as late as possible to ensure the cylinder peak pressure is reached well past 20deg after TDC. At the time peak burn pressure is reached, the piston has begun fast acceleration, thereby enlarging the combustion space. Cylinder pressure quickly tapers off as the fire chases the piston down the cylinder, which wards off harmful detonation – but also reduces horsepower.
However, combustion slows so much that as the exhaust valves open, the fire is still going. This increases exhaust valve temps and the exhaust side of the chamber becomes hotter along with the piston crown.
After this the inlet port opens and allows fresh fuel and air to enter but all the added heat affects the air charge, and it quickly expands, filling the chamber with low density air and leads to lost horsepower at best.
At worst, combustion continues on the down stroke and the piston crown, exhaust valve, and chamber have insufficient time to cool and soon reach dangerous temps and causes combustion occurs long before the plugs get fired. The intense heat generated by this pre-ignition situation acts like a blow torch and melts through the crown of the piston.

4.9 Spark Plugs

Spark Plug Heat Range
- The hotter the engine, the colder the plug range.

With any modified engine the correct heat range sparkplug must be used. You cannot keep using the manufacturer recommended plug.
A hot plug is used to avoid fouling in engines with low combustion temps. A cold plug is used to avoid overheating when temps are high – racing engines etc..
The length of the insulator nose and the electrode alloy composition are the primary determinants. Hot plugs have long noses.
Engines in sports tune will need plugs one or two steps colder than standard. More heavily tuned road engines may require two distinct plug types, one for everyday use and another colder set for hard use. Ideally rally cars should have one set of plugs for warm up and another set for maximum power driving. Otherwise use the hottest retracted-gap racing plug available. Never race while the warm up plugs are fitted.
Examining the nose of the plug will tell you if it is in the collect temperature range for your engine (the AFR must be set correctly first). Always begin testing with overly cold plugs and build up to the warmest plug that is suitable for your state of tune. You must run the engine at maximum load and then abruptly cut the ignition (this wont do the turbo any favours, but as a once off exercise it shouldn't overly wear the turbo). Once you have established the heat range, stick with this. If you are moving to another manufacturer of spark plug then you have to do the exercise over again, you cant depend on that manufacturers heat range to be calibrated the same.
This is why tuners stick to certain brands… not only because of the quality of the plug but because the heat range numbers used are spaced well and there is enough spread across the heat ranges to accommodate the engine in different states of tune.

- **Normal** – Insulator nose white or very light tan. Little or no cement boil where centre electrodes protrude through insulator nose. Electrodes not discoloured or eroded.
- **Too Cold** – Insulator nose dark grey or black Steel plug shell end covered with dry, black soot deposit that will rub off easily.
- **Too Hot** – Insulator nose chalky white or may have satin sheen. Excessive cement boil where centre electrode protrudes through insulator nose. Cement may be milk white or meringue like. Centre electrode may be blue and rounded off at edges. Earth electrode may be badly eroded or have molten appearance.
- **Pre-Ignition** – use colder plugs and remove combustion chamber deposits. Insulator nose blistered. Centre electrode and side electrode burned or melted away.
- **Detonation** – retard ignition and richen mixture. Fractured insulator nose in sustained or extreme cases. Insulator nose covered in tiny pepper specks or even tiny beads of aluminium leaving the piston. Excessive cement boil where centre electrode protrudes through insulator nose. Specks on plug shell end.
- **Insulator Glazing** – replace with plugs of same heat range. If condition persists fit plugs one grade colder. Shiny yellow, green or tan deposits on insulator nose, particularly close to centre electrode.
- **Ash Fouled** – clean or replace with plugs of the same heat range. Thick yellow, white or light brown deposit on insulator, centre and side electrode.

Electrode Material and Gap Style
- For forced induction a thick earth electrode is best.
- There are several competing designs and heat ranges.

For forced induction engines a plug with a thick earth electrode that will conduct heat away quickly must be used. A thin electrode made of poor metal quality will melt or will glow like a glow plug and cause pre-ignition.
When burning methanol, we cant use platinum electrodes because they act as a catalyst.

The projecting nose or projecting core plug is the best one to use, with copper implants in both electrodes to increase heat transfer rates. It has a wide heat range and will resist fouling and pre-ignition. At high rpms the insulator nose is cooled by incoming fuel and at low rpm it runs hot to prevent fouling. However, projecting nose plugs shouldn't be used on very high boost engines or on engines running 20% or more nitro.
If you change from a regular plug to a projecting nose type you may have to retard the ignition very slightly because the flame travel is reduced.

The next best plug is the conventional gap plug. It is usually available in colder grades than the projecting nose plug. It has a wider heat range and provides better ignition flame propagation.

For highly supercharged engines use the retracted-gap racing plug in the coldest grades available. This plug type must only be used when absolutely necessary because it tends to foul easily and it generates a poor ignition flame front.

The fine wire plug is sometimes suitable for fast road engines. It was originally developed for two stroke engines, but can be used in 4stroke engines when a wide heat range is required. They are expensive but work well when low speed fouling is a problem. They are not suitable for high boost or nitro assisted engines.

Lastly, make sure that there is physical space for the plug in the cylinder chamber. Also make sure the plug reach is not too long or too short. Exposed threads in the combustion chamber can become hot spots. These factors should be checked with the head removed or by using an identical head.

Spark Plug Gap
- - Increased power and compression will necessitate narrower gaps.
- - Upgrading the ignition system will allow wider gaps to be used.

The coil saturation time, the compression ratio and the engine speed all dictate what the spark plug gap should be.
Increasing compression and engine speed, and reducing the saturation time will all lead to the gap being made narrower and vice versa.
All modified engines retaining the stock ignition system and operating at higher than normal revs will require a narrower spark plug gap. A wide gap improves engine idle and low speed performance on lean mixtures. But at high rpms and load the ignition system is not able to provide a sustained spark across the same gap and so it must be narrowed in order to avoid high speed misfires and possible breakdown or the high-voltage system insulation. Rally engines may need a gap as low as 0.03in with conventional plugs or a gap of 0.025in with retracted-gap racing plugs. Engines running methanol will need gaps of 0.005in to initially burn it and keep it burning.
Engines with a capacitor discharge ignition system can use the original manufacturers gap for short special stages, but for longer staged events and for international rallies with restricted service intervals, a maximum gap of 0.045in should be used to avoid complete CD failure during the event. The closer plug gap reduces the load on the spark box. If trouble arises the system should survive to the end of the event.

Coil Polarity

- The spark should always jump from the centre to the outside.

Up to 40% of the energy potential is lost when the polarity on the coils reversed. The spark should always jump from the centre electrode to the outside electrode. The polarity can be checked by looking at the coils low voltage connections or by using an oscilloscope.

Spark Plug Maintenance

The plugs need to be filed, gapped and tested every 5000mls. Retracted gap plugs cannot be filed and fine wire plugs should never be filed. Projecting nose and conventional plugs should have the earth electrode bent back enough to allow filing of the sparking surface. This lowers the voltage potential requires to create a spark because the impedance is reduced and because electricity will jump a sharp edge more easily. Filing removes the dead metal and re-exposes the highly conductive material.
Never use a wire brush and don't use a 'plug cleaner'. Don't bother cleaning the plug. If its overly dirty then use a toothbrush and some non-oily solvent, otherwise just throw it away and use new plugs.

Spark Plug Leads

- Use inductive suppression leads.
- Use diameter of 8mm or more silicon wires.

Most road cars use radio suppression cables with a carbon impregnated rayon cord to conduct the high-voltage current to the spark plugs. With age the electrical resistance of these type cables increases so they should be replaced regularly or preferable discarded altogether. High quality inductive suppression leads should be used instead. These have a metal core to conduct full electrical energy to the plugs, they have a metal induction spiral wound within the cable to provide noise and induction suppression. Inadequate suppression will affect the EMU and other electronic devices. Never use ordinary copper or stainless steel core cables.
Inductive spiral leads also reduce inductive crossfire. Inductive crossfire in its mildest form causes rough running. In its worst form it will result in severe engine damage – same as severe pre-ignition.
This problem should not be taken lightly. It is not a rare occurrence on competition engines running powerful CD systems.
A crossfire on a blown engine will destroy the cylinder walls, pistons, bearings, cranks, heads and if you're lucky the head gasket. This kind of severe damage due to crossfire is most common in v8s because of the firing order of the cylinders, but it can and does happen on all configurations....
As well as using high quality leads, each lead should be separated by an inch and should never be clipped using metal clips. On v8s, consecutively firing leads(such as No's 5 and 7) should be crossed once to cut out any inductive cross firing.
Also keep the leads away from other metals by about an inch.

The average race engine needs up to 35000v to operate at optimal levels. To work in this environment use a minimum of 8mm silicone wire with plug gaps not greater than 0.028in and a max of 12psi boost. At gaps of 0.04in and boost levels beyond 15psi only the best grades of ignition wire must be used 9 or 10mm wire must be used. Alternatively, use 8mm Moroso spiral core wire with a dielectric insulation strength of well over 50kv. This combines the highest levels of electro-magnetic suppression with the least electrical resistance to ensure max ignition energy at the spark plug.

4.10 Distributor Cap and Rotor Arm

The distributor cap, rotor arm and coil tower are other areas where high-voltage leakage and flashover can occur. Keep these areas free of moisture, grime and dust. Inspect for cracks and carbon build-up.
However, don't scrape or sand the distributor cap terminals or the rotor arm contact because you will remove the insulating glaze and cause leakage to earth.
Caps and arms should be made of high quality alkyd material.
Also be wary of flashover on 6 and 8cyl engines because the high-voltage posts are very close to on another.

4.11 Primary Voltage and Ignition Performance

- Consider the entire electrical system and loom.

Power being consumed by the ignition system has an affect on the other electrical systems in the car. Electronic fuel injection, electric fuel pumps, fans and air con all place heavy loads on the electrical system and high energy CD systems can tip the balance past the levels that the alternator, wiring loom etc.. can handle. This can lead to reliability issues and engines cutting out for no apparent reason.
CD systems can have a current draw that's three times as high as a simple HEI system. Up to 10amps can be required.
The draw from HEI systems is much lower, but the instantaneous amp draw when the module is first switched to charge the coil, is very high. Therefore, a HEI system must be wired directly to the ignition switch using 10 gauge wire. Additionally, this surge can cause the EMU to shut down if its not setup correctly.

5. Boost Control and Anti-Lag

5.1 Electronic Boost Control

- Easily the best method of boost control.
- Allows an overboost facility.

Electronic control is by far the best method of boost control and provides many advantages over all other methods. With no disadvantages.

The most common method is by electronically controlling the signal line boost return. A solenoid valve is installed in the signal line and controlled by the EMU. The pulsing of this valve determines how much signal line boost is bled off.

If the knock sensor doesn't detect detonation then the pulses are spread far apart and vice versa.

An overboost facility is made possible because of this valve. A 10% boost increase is permitted of a few seconds to improve acceleration. Highly accurate actuator control is also made possible because of the electronic control valve. The valve can be kept constant until and instant before max boost and then it's kept fully open to force the actuator instantly open.

There is a danger here because the temptation is there to delay opening the actuator until the last second. This causes the same problem as having a near square cam lobe acting on an inlet or exhaust valve. Rather than opening progressively, the actuator is slammed open and starts bouncing and reverberating in an uncontrollable manner. A progressive response is a better way to go. The amount of signal bleed off trails actual boost pressure by 30% as soon as 70% of max boost is attained. By the time 90-95% of max boost is reached the actuator should be fully opened.

Overboost Protection

To protect from electronic valve failure, actuator seizure or user misuse, a backup safety valve is usually used.

The first valves to be used were simple pop-up valves that were similar to a radiator cap. Later, electronic devices were used to limit ignition or fuel when an overboosted situation occurred. There are overboost defencers on the market to overcome these restrictors (e.g. HKS overboost defencer).

If a fuel cut does occur, take your foot of the gas immediately otherwise you will destroy the engine due to an over lean situation occurring.

5.2 Anti Lag Strategy

- On short strokes and V config engines, using two smaller turbos is better.
- Some straight six engines will benefit from a sequential twin setup.
- Fuel can be dumped into the exhaust during off-throttle periods.
- Bigger turbos mean bigger turbo lag.
- Smaller turbos will reduce turbo lag but will also reduce max possible boost.

Turbo lag is always a consideration when dealing with turbos. The bigger the turbo, the more extreme the turbo lag. Big power will always mean big turbos and more exhaust energy is required to turn bigger compressors.

There are various ways to overcome turbo lag. These methods are referred to as anti lag strategies. In its most basic form, an engine management system dumps excess fuel into the engine while the driver lifts from the throttle. At the same time, it retards the ignition which causes the fuel to pass straight through the engine and into the exhaust system. When the fuel hits the turbine wheel it ignites because the wheel is at close to 1000dec Celsius. The resulting burn causes a lot of black smoke, but it rapidly accelerates the turbine wheel so that it is close to full boost when the driver reapplies the throttle.
Another approach is to place a fuel injector onto the exhaust manifold and inject directly into the exhaust manifold.
For a brief time, Ferrari used a system which virtually eliminated turbo lag. The inlet and exhaust manifolds were linked via a bypass passage containing a valve which opened as the throttle was closed. Any time the driver lifted from the throttle, compressed air from the inlet manifold rushed into the turbo. With excess fuel available, and a rush of air into the red hot turbine, enormous flow was created which quickly accelerated the turbine. However, the turbine wasn't up to dealing with the excessive forces and often failed under this pressure.

More sophisticated and fundamental strategies exist for minimising turbo lag.
For certain engines, using two or more smaller turbos rather than a single larger turbo can improve engine response and lessen turbo lag. This is particularly effective on very short stroke engines or on v configuration blocks where the exhaust outlet exits on both sides of the block.
On longer stroke engines using a single turbo can be better because there is already decent torque available in low down rpm. In this case the use of split pulse turbine housings provides superior response and spool-up time. The use of two turbos in this instance only increases complexity and weight, without giving enough improvement to justify multiple turbos. In some cases, race teams go from the production two-turbo setup to a single turbo setup.
Towards the end of the turbo F1 era, manufacturers such as KKK, Garrett and IHI were able to supply variable geometry turbines which could survive in very hostile petrol engine racing conditions. Variable geometry turbines help performance right through the rev range. At low rpm they function like a small turbo, but as rpm increases, they act like a larger turbo, allowing large amounts of boost to be generated. Previously, this technology was limited to low temp diesel turbos. The use of silicon nitrate enabled these turbos to operate at 1170deg Celsius and at over 160000 rpm.

5.3 Anti Lag in Rallying

- Group A rallying greatly refined anti-lag techniques.
- Fuel afterburn and EMU control were used.
- Easy to cook the turbo using this technique.

During the Group B era in rallying(1980s), the same strategies as mentioned above were used to limit turbo lag, however, when Group B was banned and 34mm restrictors were made mandatory, turbo lag became a serious problem, which could not be dealt with by simple ignition retard. Overcoming the problem involved careful turbo matching, new turbo design and effective anti lag systems which did not compromise turbo reliability or overly affect fuel consumption.

Before the Group A and WRC era, turbos could only sustain temperatures of around 950deg, but the introduction of better alloys and ceramics, meant turbos could now operate above 1000degrees(up to 1250deg for short periods). This opened the possibility of using fuel afterburn to keep the turbo spinning. There are a few different ways of doing this and it can sometimes depend as much on driver preference as anything else. Some drivers prefer instant response as soon as they get back on the throttle; others require a more progressive approach to anti lag, especially on forestry or gravel stages. This is one of the reasons forestry cars often require different maps to tarmac cars. The same car can require up to 5 different maps just to deal with the different antilag requirements of competitors who compete in the national forestry and national and international sealed surface events.
A simple antilag system for a rally or road car will instruct the EMU to increase fuelling by 15% when it senses a trailing throttle(less than ¼ open) at greater than 2000rpm. The EMU will than revert to 10deg before TDC and will cut spark at each cylinder by ¾.
(MoTeC and Gems units automate some of these settings).
At the same time, a suitably modified EGR valve opens in response to an EMU command linking the EGR to the inlet vacuum reservoir. Air which is under pressure from the compressor side of the turbo is forced into the exhaust manifold. Here, close to the turbine, the burst of air causes the unburned fuel to ignite.
This combustion creates heat and pressure which spools the turbo to produce over 20 psi boosts with the throttle closed.
As the throttle is reopened at the exit of the corner, boost quickly drops to about 8psi. Once past ¼ throttle, the EMU discontinues antilag operations and normal operation resumes.

5.4 Turbo Lag on Road Cars

- Great improvements in the past five years.
- Turbo lag almost eliminated on latest high compression, low boost cars.
- Turbo sizing and good gear matching have helped.

Turbo lag is becoming less and less of a problem on road cars because of better electronic control improved turbo design, but it is still a factor which must be considered on road car applications and it is an essential consideration of any competition engine setup.
And tuning beyond the stock setup leaves way for turbo lag to become a serious problem. In an effort to reach maximum top end horsepower, the lower down power and turbo lag can suffer and become even worse than stock. No improvements in top end power should be applied if it grossly affects low down response. On average a turbo car must have 30% better overall power over a naturally aspirated car just to keep a level footing on a twisty road or a race track because of the sacrifices that are made lower down the rev range. Add to this the fact that a turbo car requires more driver skill to keep it in the power zone and the need for an effective anti lag strategy becomes clearer still.
There are four main areas that have to be addressed to combat lag:
- engine hardware choice
- fine tuning fuel and spark (incl. antilag fuel and spark strategy)
- gearbox ratios and final drive ratio
- turbo sizing and technology choices

5.5 Launch Control

- Spark cut to one cylinder at a time.
- Boost is built up at the line by passing unburnt fuel to the turbine.
- Very easy on the turbo.
- Not so easy on the drive train.

A good launch strategy is essential to overcome turbo lag at the start line. A rev limit set to anything from 4000 to maximum revs is employed through a wheel mounted switch or through the clutch pedal. When the throttle is floored and the clutch is fully depressed, the launch limit is in effect and the engine will not pass the set rev limit. Spark is cut to one cylinder at a time to hold the engine revs. With spark alternatively being held from the plugs, unburned fuel is passed into the exhaust along with the air from the cylinder. Once in the exhaust manifold, the hot air/fuel mix ignites and drives the turbo turbine. Because spark isn't retarded using this method, the exhaust gases are kept reasonably cool. Therefore, afterburn combustion is slow and incomplete, so turbo temps don't reach dangerous levels.

Soft Rev Limit Control
- A more sympathetic alternative to anti-lag.
- Launch control on the move.

Sometimes you can leave the launch control on during hard driving and use it instead of the much more severe anti-lag (Motec and Gems) system employed by grpA and WRC rally cars.
Each time the clutch is depressed at engine rpm higher than the set rev limit, the turbo runs in afterburn mode. The turbo is able to maintain its speed during gear change. Along with the afterburn, the throttle is kept open and air is free to course into the engine from the compressor (rather than hitting a closed throttle plate), which allows the compressor to coast more freely. This system is so effective that a bigger/heavier turbo can actually be an advantage because of the flywheel effect keeping the compressor turning.
Along with the benefits to acceleration, there is also a benefit in that the drive never has to lift off the throttle during up or down shifts. This means you don't have to worry about heel and toeing into and out of the corner. The rev limiter will hold the revs at safe levels.

Proper Engine Tuning
- Good fuel and ignition mapping is essential.
- Turbo matching is important.
- All setup needs to be done on the dyno with diagnostic and monitoring equip.

There is no point spending thousands of euros on components without setting up the fuelling and spark to take advantage and to optimize the install. Dynoing the engine management system to get the fuelling and spark right throughout the entire rev range at all engine loads is essential.
Turbo lag can be as much a product of poor tuning as incorrect turbo sizing, wrong cams etc.
A replacement EMU or a piggyback ECU that woks in series with the existing EMU is essential when carrying out any mods to your car. The engine must be supplied with the additional air and fuel as well as having the capability to use MAF or MAP or throttle position sensors to meter AFR.

6. Water Injection

- Used to stop detonation and allow more aggressive ignition advance.
- Used extensively in competition engines.
- Requires careful mapping.

Water injection was first used on tractors and industrial engines in the 1920s to avoid detonation. It received widespread use during WW2 in American war planes and has been employed ever since for engines which need to operate at the peak of power and efficiency.

When the speed at which the fuel burns, or the speed at which the cylinder pressure rises, gets out of control the fuel mixture will explode uncontrollably causing detonation. Mild detonation will destroy head gaskets and wild detonation will quickly destroy pistons, conrods and cylinder walls, bearings, cranks and everything else in the engine !!

However, in order to extract max power and economy from an engine, we must find a balance as close as possible to the point of detonation, without crossing the line.

To eliminate detonation we must limit combustion speed and pressure rise in as gradual a way as possible so as to preserve max power and economy. One way to so this is to improve the knock resistance of the fuel but this is rarely possible for road use.

This leaves us with the option to either cut down on power and economy(no thanks) or to use some form of water injection.

Water injection isn't about dumping water into the cylinders. If power is important then water flow and atomization must be carefully controlled to provide the ideal quantity and delivery to stop detonation. Installing a cheap and crude water injection system into a car is the same as choosing carbs over fuel injection. You should never install any system based on substandard parts like windscreen washer pumps and nozzles operated by some kind of pressure switch. At best this kind of system will only prevent detonation. It won't promote more power or economy and will probably reduce power and contribute to premature cylinder wall ware by contaminating the oil supply.

An entry level water injection system should be electronically controlled with a variable pump controlled according to boost and rpm inputs as a minimum. The knock control should be altered or removed to stop spark retard or boost limiting.

A flow meter for water and fuel is also helpful to maintain a ratio of 35% of water to fuel flow(by weight). In volume terms this is 28%. The higher the intake temp and the lower the octane rating then the more water that will be required to maintain spark advance(and therefore power and economy).

On a normal road engine running 95octane fuel you should see a 5% increase in power and a 15deg drop in intake temps. Obviously if you have much higher intake temps than normal(eg.100deg) and worse fuel, you will experience even more gains by using water injection.

When we inject water it gets converted to steam, which pulls heat out of the combustion process, slowing the rate of pressure rise. These steam particles separate the fuel and oxygen molecules which further slow combustion and pressure rise. As this is happening, the piston is continuing to go to TDC, squeezing the gases tighter but with less heat in the chamber, detonation is avoided. As the piston descends a controlled burn occurs.

6.1 Proper Water Injection Systems

- Expensive and must be mapped carefully on the dyno.

Sophisticated water injection systems can be hard to justify because of the high cost involved. But for max horsepower and max engine protection from detonation then a top of the line water injection system is necessary. Such systems employ water nozzles in each inlet port and a high pressure pump delivering water at 90psi to maximize atomization. A fully programmable ECU must also be used to map the system according to boost and rpm load, compressor discharge temp and engine temp, turbo temp and overboost.

Nozzle Location
- Equal water distribution and vaporization is essential.

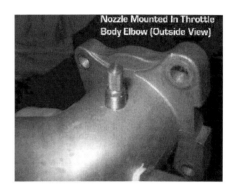

It is important to equally distribute the water haze across the chamber. This is why top end systems employ one nozzle per cylinder... but you can get close with one or two nozzles. If we are using an intercooler the nozzles are best located in the cooler outlet pipe. The turbulence here will help to disperse the water uniformly in the charge air. This also leaves plenty of time for proper mixing before the inlet. If the charge air is still hot after the intercooler it will help in vaporizing the water(which will draw heat out of the charge air early).

In non-intercooled systems, nozzle position varies depending on the type or blower or turbo being used. For centrifugal blowers and all turbos put the nozzle in the compressor outlet. With other types of blowers its better to inject into the blower intake(if excessive amounts of water are used then the blower will be damaged). However, the big gaps in roots blowers between the rotors and the case are reduced when water injection is used so we have an increase in boost and a drop in charge temperatures. Too much water will tighten the gap too much and put excessive pressure on the rotors.

6.2 Water and Alcohol Mix

- Used a lot in street-racing and sometimes in competition.. not good for the engine.

Some people advocate the use of a 50/50 water/alcohol mix. The alcohol adds a fuel value to the mix and aids further in dispersal and atomization. However, it leaves a powdery residue on aluminium and causes corrosion of piston ring lands, the rings themselves and the bore walls by washing away oil.

Water and Methanol Mix
- Much better than alcohol, use between 30 and 50% mix of methanol.
- Can be very poisonous, don't allow skin exposure.

Another option is to use a 50/50 water/methanol mix. This has similar benefits as alcohol without the downsides. Better results can sometimes be got by using a 70/30 mix. But methanol is very poisonous and can cause blindness and cancer and eventually death if it's not handled with respect. Never allow skin exposure, never inhale methanol fumes etc...

Toluol Mix
- Too expensive and rare.

Toluol can be used instead of water and has excellent resistance to detonation. But is mega expensive.

7. Fuel Types

- 95 octane is normally used; anything above this can yield more power.
- A great way to get more power for short term use.
- Must be accompanied by a remap, otherwise, less power may result.

Fuel options in this country are a bit limited. In most areas there are no options outside of 95octane pump fuel. Some stations provide 97octane.
However, for rallying and other formulas such as drag racing or for track days using road cars, there is a wealth of options available from octanes from 98 up to 120octane and above.
Most competitors and enthusiasts have probably heard of using high octane petrol, methanol and nitro methane (nitro), but this is only a small sample of the wide variety of fuels available for occasional use.

Fuel Octane Rating

- A measure of a fuels anti-knock capabilities.
- Is not a measure of power potential.

People sometimes think that a fuels octane rating is a measure of its power output. This is not true. In fact changing from 95 octane to 98 octane in a normal road car, without remapping the ignition map, will probably result in a power loss !!
Without a remap or without a knock management system, there is no way for an engine to take advantage of increased octane ratings.

Octane rating is in fact a measure of a fuels anti-knock capabilities. The higher the octane rating, the more resistant the fuel is to knocking. The likelihood of damaging detonation and pre-ignition occurring is lessened by using higher octane fuel. When the engine is remapped to take advantage of this anti-knock characteristic then more power is produced.

History of Octane Standards

At the start of WW1, there was no such thing as an octane rating for fuel. However, it was found that highly tuned engines in cars and planes reacted differently to different batches of fuel that was thought to be identical. Two tins of fuel, both from the same refinery and both with identical weights etc.. would react differently in the engine. The engine would run well on one tank of fuel and when it was refilled it would blow up while running on the other batch of fuel.

The labs weren't able to distinguish between a good and bad batch of fuel. To overcome this problem, special single piston fuel research engines were made and distributed to different labs around the world. The labs would test the quality of the fuel by running the engine on the fuel and raising the compression ratio until knocking occurred. This was called the HUCR rating(Highest Usable Compression Ratio).
To calibrate the engines before testing, two pure fuel substitute substances were used to establish a high and low reference point. The high reference fuel used was isooctane(2-2-4 trimethylpentane) and the low reference fuel was heptane(n-heptane).

The following method was then used to determine a fuels quality.
Firstly, its HUCR was determined as mentioned previously.
Then various runs would be carried out using different mixes of the high and low reference fuels, iso-octane and n-heptane until a blend was found that had a knock behaviour identical to the knock behaviour of the fuel under test. Then the fuel under test would be rated according to the percentage of iso-octane and n-heptane used.
So a fuel that behaved the same as 95%_iso-cotane and 5%_n-heptane would be rated at 95 octane petrol. This is how octane ratings came into widespread use.

Research and Motor Tests

*   Research test, or RON measures the fuels low RPM performance.
*   Motor test, or MON measures the fuel high RPM performance.
*   MON is more relevant for forced induced engines.

Newer research and motor tests have come into widespread use. The same basic methods and test engines are still used, but a new test call the motor octane test has more relevance than the older(but more widespread) research octane test.
The motor method uses the same engine, but runs it at a higher rpm and intake temperature and gets the octane figure based on these conditions – therefore, this test is more relevant to forced induction engines.

To repeat, the MON(Motor Octane Number) is more relevant for highly stressed engines than the RON(Research Octane Number) but it is the RON number often gets quoted at. This is because, for the same fuel, the RON number will always be higher than the MON number, and it sounds better to quote the RON number.

Use the MON number to indicate the knock resistance at high load and RPM.
Use the RON number to indicate the knock resistance at part load and lower RPM.

The difference between the RON and MON is called the fuels sensitivity.
A typical batch of fuel could have a RON of 95 and a MON of 85. This means that the fuel has an octane rating of 95 at low load and an octane rating of 85 at high load.
The next batch of fuel could have the same RON of 95 with a MON of 88. Obviously this fuel will be better at high engine load even though the RON is the same.

High Octane Test

*   High octane test, or SON tests for octanes over 100 octane.

Any fuels which have an octane rating that is higher than 100 have a different test called the Supercharge test(obviously the traditional tests won't work on fuels greater than 100 octane).
The Supercharge Octane Numbers(SON) is got by extending the old system in a linear fashion beyond 100.
In this test the high reference fuel used is iso-octane with lead additives.
Two tests are carried out, the F3 and F4 tests.
The F3 test is done at cruise and the F4 test is done using full load.
This is why high octane fuels have two numbers e.g. 100/130.

Avgas Race Fuel

*   Used for aviation and competition.

Most of the older racing fuels are actually Avgas fuels rebadged as racing fuel. 'Racing 115' fuel is in fact 'Avgas 115/145'. Leaded 'Racing 100' is the same as 'Avgas 100/130'. The old green Avgas was used as leaded 108 racing fuel and the newer blue Avgas was used as unleaded 108 racing fuel.
Recently, Avgas 112/160 has been launched as 'Racing 108' leaded fuel.

Dedicated Motorsport Fuels

*   Aviation fuel tailored for motorsport use or originally derived for motorsport.

A lot of the big companies produce fuels specifically for motorsport use. These fuels are designed to give the anti-knock capabilities of Avgas with improved throttle response and power. Typically, 4-5% at the top end and more at the midrange.
In the USA VP Motorsport 103 is very popular(99MON, 107RON, 3%oxygen). One of the top fuels in USA is Power-Mist RFG(104MON, 112RON, 6%oxygen).
Formula 1 fuel is also top class, but it is somewhat limited by the regulations. F1 fuel has a maximum RON or 102 and max oxygen content of 2.7% and is made up of Toluol, xylene, sopentane, iso-octane, hexene-1, n-butane, 2-methylpentane.

Octane Boosters

- Selected brands are effective, but some brands have little effect.

As mentioned, Toluol and xylene are the main anti-knock agents in F1. In the past, a good way to increase the anti-knock properties of petrol was to add Toluol to the petrol(up to 33%). However, it can't be used on unleaded fuel as a reliable octane booster.

The most effective octane booster is MMT(methyl cyclopentandienyl manganese tricarbonyl). It is used in NF Racing Formula and Nulon Pro Strength. They will both add 3ron to 95ron fuel and 1.5ron to 98ron fuel.

Most other octane boosters are less effective. You have to check the contents carefully to see if it contains any usable chemicals. Also, most of the claims made on the package are usually not true.

Methanol

- Very high latent heat of vaporization allows big power gains up to 20%.
- Requires revised fuel delivery.

A fuels octane rating is not the whole story. There are many factors that contribute to a fuels power potential. Methanol has a MON of 90 yet can produce power increases of 20% over petrol.
Shell 'A' racing fuel is 96% methanol and 3% acetone. The key to methanol is its very high latent heat of vaporization. It takes a lot of heat to be converted from liquid to vapour. Petrol has 135Btu/lb. whereas methanol has 472Btu/lb. The heat required for proper atomization is drawn from the piston crown, inlet tract, combustion chamber and inlet and exhaust valves. This results in an internally cooler engine which puts less heat into the inlet charge, so the charge density goes up and the horsepower goes up.
Another factor acting in methanol's favour is the amount of energy available in the burned fuel. Using petrol, the best power ratio is around 13:1. With methanol the air/fuel ratio for max power is about 5:1. Because were consuming much more methanol, were also absorbing more heat from the engine. (Note: this means we need to flow double the amount of methanol – bigger fuel lines, bigger fuel pumps, bigger injectors etc...).

The major downside to using methanol is that it is extremely poisonous. It can slowly build up inside of you and cause blindness and insanity. It can be absorbed through the skin and lungs. It is also present in the burnt exhaust gas especially in rich burning mix.

It can also be damaging to your engine. It will eat through fibreglass resin. It has a scouring effect on tanks and fuel lines. It will absorb huge amounts of water so it must be kept airtight. After use the whole system has to be flushed out with petrol. It promotes water induced rust and corrosion inside the engine. It is particularly damaging to aluminium and zinc. It regularly leads to blocked injectors. Methanol does not lubricate like petrol, so flat-slide and barrel-type throttles tend to stick on methanol. In colder climates starting problems will be experienced. Methanol burns much more slowly than petrol so the ignition needs to be advanced.

Nitro Methane
- Can double the power output.
- Used on drag cars.

Nitro methane doesn't even have an octane
rating because it is too variable, yet it can more
than double a petrol engines power. This is
because extremely rich mixtures can be used
and because of its unique chemical makeup.
Nitro methane contains 53% oxygen so it permits
large quantities of fuel for conversion to heat energy.
Because it burns so slowly, it keeps pushing the piston
to the bottom of the stroke.

Nitro used to be mixed with methanol for use in drag racing, but nowadays nitro is used with almost no methanol blended in.
It is necessary to reduce the compression ratio in engines to protect against detonation. The air/fuel mix must always be set very rich, sometimes 2:1.
Igniting nitro is always a problem. Dragsters use 1.2 amps in each plug. 50deg advance is used.

Nitro methane is equally or more dangerous than methanol. After combustion, the vapour contains large amounts of nitric acid, which causes muscle reaction and prevents a person from breathing, so gas masks are essential to survive.
Nitro on itself is not explosive.

Other Fuels
Petrol, methanol and nitro methane can have various compounds added to them.

Propylene oxide(epoxy propane) is used with nitro to increase combustion flame speed. It can also be used with petrol and methanol to give 2-3% power gain. It must be stored in plastic or aluminium containers because it becomes volatile when in contact with copper or rust.

Nitro propane can be added to any fuel to increase the oxygen content. Obviously, serious remapping must be done afterwards.

All of the above additives must be used in specific mixes and there are a host of precautions which must be practiced when mixing them…. There is not enough scope here to go through the details, but like any chemicals, you shouldn't use them without discussing it with an experienced tuner or chemist.

Real World Effects of Octane Increase
On a highly tuned two litre turbo(Scooby, Evo, GT4) the following can be expected.
If the engine is running at 400bhp on 98RON fuel then the use of 101 Shell clubman fuel will bring the engine to 450bhp due to the added boost and advance allowed because of the octane increase. With a further increase to 102 WRC fuel and the use of Toluol additive to bring the MON to 113octane, the engine will produce just over 500bhp(at 9psi boost higher than the 98octane level).

8. Engine Management Fundamentals

First take note of the two items essential to fundamental tuning:

Fuel Tuning
A wideband lambda meter is essential for fuel tuning.
No point in tuning the fuel table if you don't know what your mixtures are at. Alternative ways of estimating the fuel mixture and verifying the lambda meter is working OK is by looking at the exhaust gas and by checking the colour of the spark plug tips.

Ignition Tuning
If you can't hear detonation in the engine then you should use a suitable detonation detector.
Never tune the ignition table if you have no way of determining when detonation is occurring.

Tuning Fundamentals
Using a good lambda probe and detonation detector, you can successfully map the fuel and ignition tables. However, to get the maximum out of your tuning it will be necessary to check your efforts on a dyno.

Coolant temperature sensors must be used to keep tabs on the temperature of the engine.
Ideal setups will also have up to three engine oil temperature sensors. One at the sump, another at the oil filter housing (or elsewhere at the mid point in the block) and another towards the top of the block(usually at the highest external oil pipe).
Exhaust gas temperature sensors are also a good aid to tuning. Again, ideal setups will employ three EGT sensors. One in the manifold, one in the mid section and another at the back of the exhaust. Individual cylinder tuning will require a EGT in each manifold runner. Remember that temperatures as low as 760degC can cause valve seats to lift.
If you are using the road instead of a dyno, then an accelerometer is an essential bit of kit.
If you are tuning on the dyno, then remember that the engine will always run a litter leaner on the dyno. If you don't take this into account then you will be running too rich on the road/track and thus losing power. When tuning on the road, look out for black smoke and lazy response which will indicate a rich mixture. If you experience backfiring and coughing then you are running lean.

To avoid meltdown, start from rich and work to lean.
Always tune the engine in open loop mode. Do not allow the ECU to automatically adjust the fuel mix or the ignition advance while you are tuning.
When you have reached a reasonable level of tuning experience then you should also zero out all of the safety compensation maps before starting to tune. If you decide not to zero out these tables, then make sure you are always operating within the normal operating temperature and boost of the engine.

8.1 Air Fuel Ratio

AFR has a fundamental effect of the performance of the engine. AFR should vary according to load and octane rating of the fuel.

Rich mixtures combat knock through the intercooling effect of the excess fuel.

The chemically ideal AFR at which all fuel is burned and all air is consumed is at 14.68 to 1. This is referred to as the stoic ratio. Mixtures with a greater percentage of air are called lean mix and mixtures with more fuel are called rich.

- In Lambda the best mixture for power is lambda of 0.9.
- At high load and maximum RPM a richer mixture is preferable because it ensures that there is enough fuel present to use all the available oxygen. At this state a mix of 0.85lambda is required.
- For best driveability a mix of 0.97 to 1.05lambda is required depending on load and RPM. At higher RPMs reverse pulsing tends to enrich the mixture anyway.

The best power strategy is to ensure that there is always enough air available for the fuel. So for maximum power engine you should never have a situation where you tune the engine any leaner then 1 lambda. (The best fuel economy strategy is to make sure there is a small oxygen surplus so that every bit of fuel is burned, so mixtures equal or leaner than 1 lambda are required).

Steady State

When an engine is operating continuously as a particular load and speed it will quickly reach equilibrium and the power/torque and temperatures will stabilise. When this happens you can start tuning for that location on the map.

For best torque at wide open throttle you should aim for lambda of 0.9 to 0.87. However, by sacrificing a miniscule amount of power you can tune for a lambda od 0.92 to 0.9 and get much better fuel efficiency which is desirable for road use and for long distance competition use.

On supercharged engines maximum safe torque will be achieved at lambda 0.83.

Under high vacuum conditions you should aim for lambda of 1.02 to 1.05 or even cut the fuel altogether to prevent back firing through the exhaust.

At idle, aim for a lambda of 1, (but no higher unless you are making a temporary NCT map).

For smooth driveability all mixtures should transition smoothly from idle to part throttle right up to full throttle and full load conditions.

8.2 Fuel Mapping

Always work from rich to lean... only tune from lean to rich when you are definitely below a lambda of 1. Before starting to tune the fuel, make sure your ignition map is set to a conservative ignition retarded state.

Idle Tuning
Start by tuning at idle in open loop mode.

Aim for lambda of 1. This won't produce the absolute best idle, but it will work best with closed loop systems and it will keep the cats in good shape and is almost the best place for idle anyway.

If you are suffering from very bad reversion then use a slightly richer mixture.

If no mixture will provide a good idle (always because of very lairy cams) then you will have to use the MAP sensor or an alphaN system to achieve good idle.

If you are using a Gems or Motec ECU you can combine the MAP and alphaN systems to get good idle.

After initial idle tuning, turn on all the electrics including rear screen heater, air-con and full lights etc. and repeat the process of idle tuning. Almost all modern cars will have an IAC valve which will cut in a cause the throttle to open by about 300RPM and cause fast idle.... This will cause the indicator in the fuel table to move to another load site and you must retune in this load site. Simply copy the values you have already inputted and tweak them to get the desired AFR.

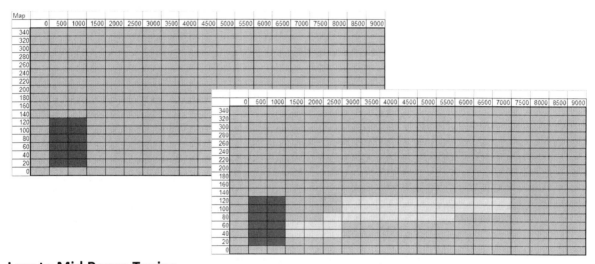

Low to Mid Range Tuning
Now apply a small amount of throttle while keeping the can in neutral. Slowly work your way into the load sites close to idle and hold in a central load site until the AFR reading and the coolant and exhaust gas temp stabilise. Now tune that site to lambda of 1(or slightly richer 0.99). Again, move to the next site and repeat the process. Keep going until all of the neutral load sites are tuned.

Return to idle and let the engine rest at idle until the temperature returns to below the thermostat setting(around 80degC). While waiting for this, start smoothing our the sites surrounding the sites you have tuned by inserting sensible values based on the values you found when tuning.

Now go on the road(or dyno) and begin to tune the load sites just above the neutral load sites. It doesn't matter what gear you use for this, but if you have a choice then use the gear that is directly matched to the drives, usually 4th in a 5 speed transmission.

Drive at a steady state and hold in as many low to mid part throttle load sites as you can and hold there until things equalise and again tune to lambda of 1 or slightly richer.

Tune all the low to mid range throttle points to a lambda of 1 to 0.99. Any sites that can't be reached but are close to other tuned sites can be guestimated using common sense.

Now pull over and give the engine another chance to cool down to 80degC. Again review the new load site settings and smooth out the surrounding untuned sites.

Before moving onto the mid range tuning sites, write in likely values based on your progress so far. For example, if the idle sites contain a value of '10' and the low to mid sites contain a value of '20' then its reasonable to assume that the mid range sites will need a value around the '30' mark. Take a good guess at what the next untuned midrange sites should contain and fill them in. By this time the engine will have returned to idle temperature and you can continue tuning at the mid range load level.

Mid Range Tuning

At medium engine loading you need to richen things up a bit. Now aim for a lambda of 0.95 to 0.92 when tuning each load site. The higher up the load range you go the less feasible it will be to try and tune every single load site. This is because it will be difficult to hone in on the required site and because you are starting to enter the upper half of the RPM band which will put extra pressure on the engine and a good tuner should aim to complete tuning while placing the engine under the minimum of pressure while achieving a good safe and exhaustive map.

Choose every second or third site and tune it to the required lambda(0.95 to 0.92), and guess at what the intervening sites should contain. Once this is done you can do a spot check to make sure all sites contain the desired lambda.

	0	500	1000	1500	2000	2500	3000	3500	4000	4500	5000	5500	6000	6500	7000	7500	8000	8500	9000
340																			
320																			
300																			
280																			
260																			
240																			
220																			
200																			
180																			
160																			
140																			
120																			
100																			
80																			
60																			
40																			
20																			
0																			

Mid to Upper Range Tuning

The higher up the load range we go the more stress we place on the engine and the more potential there is to cause damage to the engine due to over stress while operating without a complete fuel map. Therefore, once you reach the mid to upper level of load and RPM, you must become good at guessing what values should be in the next sites to be tuned. This is easier than it sounds and once you use a little experience and some common sense, you will be able to estimate to within 10% what your next values should be. Once you make sure that you err on the side for rich, you won't go far wrong.

Again, instead of trying to tune every site in the mid to upper range, only tune every third or fourth site and verify that you guess work has been reasonably accurate. If you find that you were way out, then return to idle and have another go at estimating the correct values. If you find that your estimates were fairly close and weren't overly lean then hold the engine in each load site and tune as usual, remember that it may take a little longer for the engine to stabilise within each site so wait for the coolant and exhaust gases to stabilise…. But if you notice things getting too hot then back off immediately.

The 3D graphing functionality built into most ECU software packages will help in this regard. If your software doesn't have this option then use Microsoft Excel or some other spread sheet to generate good graphs.

	0	500	1000	1500	2000	2500	3000	3500	4000	4500	5000	5500	6000	6500	7000	7500	8000	8500	9000
340																			
320																			
300																			
280																			
260																			
240																			
220																			
200																			
180																			
160																			
140																			
120																			
100																			
80																			
60																			
40																			
20																			
0																			

Maximum Throttle Tuning

Once the mid to upper tuning is complete then progress to full throttle tuning. Once again, estimate what the full throttle sites should contain…. This should be very easy, since by now you have 90% of the basic tuning of the map complete. Of course, you should keep this slightly richer than you require.

Your approach to full throttle tuning will be the same as the mid to upper range of tuning provided the engine is not prone to overheating at this level(if it is then there is probably a mechanical or other reason). If the engine is in good shape then continue with full throttle tuning by checking every third or fourth load site and tuning to a lambda of 0.89 to 0.85 and then filling in the surrounding sites with sensible values.

At this point it is a good idea to remember that in exceptional circumstances, when the engine is very prone to detonation, it may be necessary to tune the engine to abnormally rich levels of tune in order to avoid engine destruction.

Note: This may be due to bad head design, an engine problem like a melted spark plug tip or excessive boost levels.. or may just be a characteristic of the engine setup. Obviously, rather than tuning the engine to this state, the inherent problem should be addressed and fixed.

This may also be due to excessive ignition advance in the igniting table. If so go to the ignition table and remove the excessive ignition advance.

Unusable Fuel Areas

This completes the tuning of the USABLE fuel map. Next you should look at the entire table and make sure there are no sudden shifts in values from one site to the next. If there are sudden jumps in the values from one site to a neighbouring site then smooth it out and recheck it by holding the engine at both sites and checking the lambda values.

In order to tune the inaccessible areas of the map you will have to input values which continue the trend in the x and y directions of the map. You may think that there is no need to tune these sites because the engine will never reach these load sites, however there are a number to things to keep in mind. Firstly, just because you couldn't reach these load sites during tuning, doesn't mean that the customer won't reach these sites under different conditions… e.g. during different air temperatures or different terrain, like steep uphill and downhill driving. Also, if the efficiency of the engine is improved or if the boost control circuit suffers a failure then load sites that were previously inaccessible will become usable.

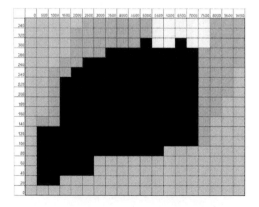

Fine Tuning the Fuel Map

If you've tuned on the dyno then remember to lean out the mixture to allow for road conditions.
High power fine tuning will always require the use of EGT sensors. The exhaust gas temperature is
unpredictable at maximum torque and should be watched carefully when tuning at full throttle. If a minor
reduction in torque results in stabilising the exhaust gas then this must be done before finishing the fuel
map. It is preferable to sacrifice a measly 1 or 2 BHP to maintain a healthy engine. Keep in mind that
excessive exhaust temperatures will not be transmitted to the coolant in time to save the engine from
destruction, so the ECU won't pick up on the problem until its too late.
Peak exhaust temperature occurs at the slightly lean side of best power and falls off after this. An exception
to this rule of thumb is when you are running excessively retarded ignition and therefore, dumping unburnt
fuel into the exhaust manifold which then ignites, causing excessive exhaust temperatures... remember that
this is not indicative of the engine combustion temperature.

Spark plug spot checking should be carried out once the fuel map is near completion. You need to run the
engine at full load and kill the engine abruptly and then remove the plugs and check the colour of the tips. If
they are black then you know that you are running rich and that your lambda probe is goosed. The plugs
should be light brown after a hard run.

Ram Air Fuel Mapping

If you are tuning a lot of drag racing cars with cold air induction kits or you are tuning superbikes or race-
cars(not rally cars), then you need to build a further Ram-Air Fuel map. Ram air effects are not present
during tuning and only occur during use after tuning so a Ram-Air Map is essential to avoid engine damage.
This is covered in the 'T5. Engine Management for Motorsport' course.

8.3 Ignition Mapping

The ignition section is shorter than the fuel section. This is because there is no point in repeating the instructions for working through the map. Bear in mind that you must proceed through the map in the same way as you do for fuel tuning…. Stopping at each load site and allowing the engine to stabilise and then adding or removing ignition as required…. Use the same procedure as fuel tuning and refer to the sections below to get a good guide as to what values you should aim for in each area of the map.

Setting the correct ignition advance across all load sites is equally important to good performance as fuel tuning.
Too much timing will result in detonation, even if the fuel map is perfectly set.
Too little timing will result in poor running and excessive exhaust gas temperatures.
If the exhaust manifold is glowing then you can be sure that you have run too little advance. If you are suffering from detonation then you are using too much advance.
All engines will require more advance at lower load conditions. Keep in mind that as you move up the load sites and across the RPM sites you will require less and less ignition.

Idle Tuning
Once again we start at idle.
At idle the engine is at its lowest load and speed and typically requires 10 to 20deg of ignition.

Once again you can tweak the ignition values to perfect idle.
If you find it very difficult to achieve even idling even with optimised fuel setup… then try removing 5 or 6 deg of ignition and this will usually kill responsiveness at idle and thus deaden the tendency of the engine to hunt at idle.

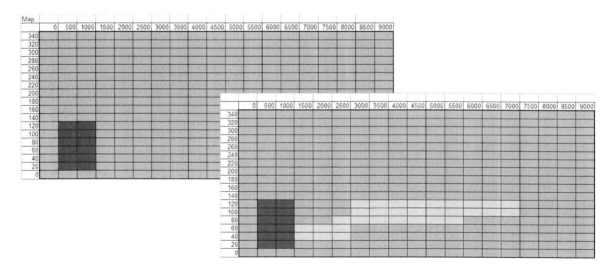

Low to Mid Range Tuning
Unlike fuel tuning, ignition tuning won't necessarily follow a linear or smooth transition from site to site. As the crank quickly accelerates out of idle, a large amount of ignition will be required to produce best torque and power and maintains good engine responsiveness.
You may need to dial in as much as 30 deg of advance in this area.

Mid Range Tuning

Moving further up the rev and load range will result in us approaching the maximum torque portion of the ignition map and therefore, we will require progressively less advance... sometimes around 20 deg. However at medium loads and low RPM we will have to reintroduce more advance to maintain responsiveness.. around 26 deg is right for this part of the ignition map.

	0	500	1000	1500	2000	2500	3000	3500	4000	4500	5000	5500	6000	6500	7000	7500	8000	8500	9000
340																			
320																			
300																			
280																			
260																			
240																			
220																			
200																			
180																			
160																			
140																			
120																			
100																			
80																			
60																			
40																			
20																			
0																			

Mid to Upper Range Tuning

In the mid to upper range, when load is low but RPMs are getting higher and higher, we will need to reach the maximum advance of the ignition table. We will need as much as 40deg advance in this area of the map(this is less true for very high compression engines).

Remember that at this point and as we progress to max throttle tuning, bigger capacity engines will require more advance than smaller power plants. Also, lower compression power plants will need a few more ignition degrees to maintain good torque. A good example of this is with the K20 Jap engine and the K20A2 UK engine. Both are identical apart from the compression ratio(and the Cams which don't feature here).

	0	500	1000	1500	2000	2500	3000	3500	4000	4500	5000	5500	6000	6500	7000	7500	8000	8500	9000
340																			
320																			
300																			
280																			
260																			
240																			
220																			
200																			
180																			
160																			
140																			
120																			
100																			
80																			
60																			
40																			
20																			
0																			

Maximum Throttle Tuning

At maximum output, the effective pressure in the cylinders is at its maximum and we must remove ignition at this point to compensate, otherwise we will suffer from lost torque and a saggy engine response. As mentioned, small capacity motors require less ignition. Engines with compression profiled pistons will also require a little less advance.

Peak torque across the entire maximum throttle load area is the aim here. Keep adding ignition until you achieve best torque. However, because we are at the maximum output of the engine we need to knock back a small amount of advance to ensure that we never exceed the maximum torque point. Normally 2degrees is sufficient.

	0	500	1000	1500	2000	2500	3000	3500	4000	4500	5000	5500	6000	6500	7000	7500	8000	8500	9000
340																			
320																			
300																			
280																			
260																			
240																			
220																			
200																			
180																			
160																			
140																			
120																			
100																			
80																			
60																			
40																			
20																			
0																			

Fine Tuning the Ignition Map

After completing the basic ignition map you should return to the fuel map and redo the fine tuning procedure. Once you have verified that everything is OK on the fuel front you car return to the ignition map and perform the final tweaking of the map.

Anything that affects engine efficiency will require fine tuning of the ignition map.

8.4 Cold Start/Accelerator Enrichment/Idle Control

Cold Start and Warm Up
Fuel molecules don't vaporise well in cold conditions. This will cause difficulties when trying to start an engine in cold conditions.
Extra fuel must be delivered to get the engine started and to keep it running during warm-up.
All ECUs will provide some method of doing this. Most of the best ECUs use cold start tables which are user configurable. You will always need to alter these tables to achieve good cold starting. You can never depend on the default values.
This is doubly true if you are using large injectors, different intake designs, long intake runners.

Cold Coolant Enrichment
Cold running enrichment increases the pulse width of the injectors by a small amount. This duration gradually reduces to zero as the engine approaches normal operating temperature.

Cold Air Enrichment
Cold air enrichment does the same thing except that it uses the intake air temperature as it's input. As the intake air heats up, the table inserts less and less fuel compensation.

Cranking Enrichment
When the engine is cranking, a cold air injector is fired(or the normal injectors pulse width is increased) to enrich the mixture to allow the engine to start. When the engine is at normal temperature is uses the zero load site in the fuel table without any cranking enrichment.

Post Start Compensation
This occurs for a fixed number of revolutions after starting and is always done automatically by the ECU. It doesn't require user input.

Idle Air Control Compensation
Simply increases the idle speed when the engine is cold so that it heats up quickly.

Obviously, before you can alter these tables, the engine must be cold, so you have to wait until the engine is stone cold and try your best not to heat it up when setting up these tables.

Engines usually require 15 to 20% enrichment when fully cold in the morning. This will then fall to 0% when approaching 70degC coolant temp. Ideally you want the ambient temperature to be as cold as possible, but of course you can't control this so you will have to estimate what the values should be when the weather is -5degC or colder. Do this be looking at what fuel you needed at +10degC, +20degC, +30degC etc... and work back in a linear fashion to estimate the colder temperatures.

Accelerator Enrichment
Accelerator enrichment and enleanment is important to maintain crisp responsiveness. Most of the default tables are set fairly close to what you will want, so you won't need to work to hard to get these tables setup. However, the more modified your engine, the more you will need to tweak the accel tables.
Naturally, the fuel table must be completely finished before attacking the acceleration enrichment tables(or any other compensation tables). In fact, all other tables should be complete before dealing with the acceleration tables.
It is used to keep the engine from stuttering when you stab the throttle and to provide as responsive as possible the reactions of the engine in reply to throttle fluctuations. The tables are based primarily on throttle position and RPM position. Some of the acceleration enrichment tables also use the MAP sensor as the load input.

Once you get used to setting up acceleration enrichment tables, you will be able to have the car setup within a mile of testing. However, when doing your first few vehicles, you will need to spend an hour or two getting the accel tables sorted.

The first thing to watch for are black smoke and deceleration flames from the exhaust. Naturally this means that the accel tables are too rich.

Adjust the tables upwards if the car is bogging down under acceleration(do most of the work below 4000RPM).

You will need to do the most work at 1200RPM to 2000RPM and less input will be required the higher up the RPM range you go. By the time you reach 6000RPM you won't need much input from the acceleration tables.

If you max out the acceleration tables and you are still having responsiveness problems or poor running then you will have to go back to the fuel table and retune it.

If you are happy that you have tuned the fuel table correctly and you have tweaked the acceleration tables to maximum and still experience running problems, then you will probably be running very large inlet runners (up to 50mm) and may need to switch some of the accel tables from throttle to MAP passed loading. In theory, this defeats the purpose of accel tables, but in practice it can solve your responsiveness issues.

Idle Control

Idle control is achieved in most vehicles by using an idle stepper motor or an idle air control valve. These systems are controlled by the ECC and are used to stabilise the engine idle at the desired level(750 to 1200RPM).

If you don't configure your idle settings/tables in the ECU then you will experience hunting at idle, which means the ECU won't react quickly enough to catch the RPMs dropping below idle, and when the ECU does detect the overly low RPMs if overreacts and causes the RPM to over rev… this cycle continues until the RPM equalises, or it will go on indefinitely if the settings are well out of sync.

It won't take long to get a good idle control setup right. However, you must make sure that the hardware side of things are setup correctly, otherwise no amount of tweaking the ECU settings will get good idle. Make sure your stepper motor is oriented correctly and your throttle Hi/Lo position is correct.

Cylinder Tuning

During normal tuning procedures we must set the fuel to be lean enough for best power, but rich enough to maintain safe engine running under all load conditions. We must also set the ignition table to be advanced enough for best power, but retarded enough to avoid engine meltdown.

For most situations this is sufficient and will result in a satisfactory tuning map that will provide good power and driveability.

However, if we want to get the absolute maximum from the engine we will need to tune each individual cylinder.

The topic of individual cylinder tuning is beyond the scope of this book. However, it is a simple procedure and the advanced engine tuner should be aware of the process.

8.5 Mapping for Modifications

This section gives recommended procedures for ECU tuning on vehicles that have the base tuning complete but require retuning due to modification that have been made to the power plant.

Always Take a Baseline

Before performing any tuning or hardware modifications, take a baseline log (and dyno run if possible) of the car's current performance. Parameters such as ignition timing, knock correction, injector duty, boost pressure, EGT and engine RPM. Once a baseline reading has been taken, subsequent modifications may be measured against the original. Before embarking on retuning the ECU, satisfy yourself that the car has no faults or problem to begin with. Check for diagnostic trouble codes and ensure any prior modifications are compatible with the work that you are going to carry out. E.g.. If a customer has requested that a larger turbo be fitted and tuned, but the up-pipe catalytic converter is still present, then it will not be safe to carry out this work.

Modifications List

Results of changes to mechanical configurations of the engine must be optimised by ECU tuning. In some circumstances, the fitting of high performance parts will reduce engine power until compensated for in the ECU – a very common example of this is induction kits. Fitting of an induction kit with no ECU compensation mapping often results in poor turbo spool up, hesitation, and lean mixtures and in extreme circumstances engine failure. However, with the same kit fitted, but with the ECU correctly mapped, will produce worthwhile power improvements with none of the problems detailed above.

In the following sections, a number of common modifications are listed. Under each heading, the parameters that may need attention are described. The ECU changes suggested are to compensate for the mechanical changes.

Under each mechanical modification heading below, the parameters to modify are split into two sections:

- The 'Compensation' section details what must be changed for correct operation. For example, changing an exhaust downpipe will cause the boost pressure to become unstable. Alteration of the waste gate duty cycle map will bring this back under control

- The 'Tuning for Power' section details what else may also be modified in order to attain further power increases. For example, removing a cat will allow the fuel mixtures to be leaned out slightly, since there is no longer a cat whose temperature must be safeguarded.

8.6 Exhaust Backbox(Muffler)/Centre Section/Downpipe Change

Compensation
- Turbo Waste gate Duty Cycle. A more free flowing exhaust requires lower waste gate duties to produce the same level of boost.
- Load Scaling of Ignition & Fuel Maps. Higher loads will be produced with a better exhaust. Fuel and ignition maps may need to be rescaled for higher loads.

Tuning for Power
After this modification, standard techniques of raising boost and advancing ignition
may be used.

Up-Pipe
SAME AS ABOVE

8.7 Induction Kits & Intake Pipes

Compensation
- Air Flow Sensor Scaling / Fuel Mapping. The correct way to compensate for an induction kit is to modify the air flow sensor scaling to correctly relate air flow sensor voltage to mass air flow. However this technique requires precise measurement of the air flow of the new induction kit. Whilst not ideal, a similar result may be obtained by filling in any holes in the fuel map by watching lambda values.
- Turbo Waste gate Duty Cycle. A freer flowing induction system will allow the turbo to spool more quickly. Waste gate duty cycles may need to be decreased to keep boost pressures under control.

Tuning for Power
After this modification, standard techniques of raising boost and advancing ignition
may be used.

8.8 Turbo

Compensation
- Turbo Waste gate Duty Cycle. The relationship between boost pressure and duty cycle required are different for each model of turbo and actuator. Duty cycles may need significant alteration to produce the desired results
- Load Scaling of Ignition & Fuel Maps. With the higher loads produced by the increased air flow of the turbo, the fuel and ignition maps will need to be rescaled.

Tuning for Power
- Boost Pressure. A higher flow turbo will be capable of higher boost pressure
- Ignition Timing. Ignition timing may be advanced, since the turbo will cause less exhaust gas restriction, decreasing EGTs.
- Fuelling. Because of the lower EGTs for a given air flow, fuelling may be able to be leaned out slightly.

8.9 Injector Change

Compensation
- Injector Scaling

Tuning for Power
- Boost Pressure. Once more fuelling capacity is available, boost pressure may be increased without compromising desired fuel mixtures.

8.10 Intercooler

Compensation
- Turbo Waste gate Duty Cycle. Freer flowing intercoolers require lower waste gate duties to produce the same level of boost, since the pressure drop across the intercooler is lower.

Tuning for Power
- Boost Pressure. Boost pressure may be increased, since a larger capacity intercooler will be more able to reduce the higher charge temperatures produced by the turbo.
- Ignition Timing. This may be advanced since charge temperatures will be lower with a larger intercooler.

8.11 Major Internal Engine Modifications

When altering the capacity, strength or cams of the engine, several parameters may need to be modified.
- Rev Limit
- Boost Pressure
- Turbo Waste gate Duty Cycle
- Ignition Timing
- Fuelling

Generally when going to this level of modification you are as well off to start from scratch and map the ECU from scratch.

8.12 Boost Related Map Values

Desired Boost

This map controls the amount of boost pressure that the ECU tries to achieve, based on RPM and throttle position. It is wise to tail off boost at high RPMs to preserve engine reliability.

When altering boost control, make small changes and data log the results. This makes it easy to see what duty cycles are being used in order to produce a given level of boost, and help determine suitable values for the maximum duty cycle map.
Note: if a log is taken, and the boost pressure reported is a flat line of e.g. 20 PSI, then this means that the boost could be much higher.
There is an alternative way of reading boost pressure that avoids this problem – log manifold absolute pressure instead. The easiest way to interpret the data is to display in units of bar, since 1 bar is approximately atmospheric pressure. At sea level, a manifold absolute pressure of 2.2 bar equates to 1.2 bar of boost pressure i.e. just subtract one and you have manifold relative pressure.

Maximum Waste gate Duty

This map controls the maximum waste gate duty that the ECU can use for a given RPM and throttle position. The values in this map must be great enough to permit the required boost to be achieved, but low enough so as not to allow over boost to occur.

Initial Waste gate Duty

Only used in the newest ECUs. This is the ECU's first guess at the correct waste gate duty, based on RPM and throttle position. The waste gate duty chosen from this map is then altered by compensation maps for atmospheric pressure, temperature and turbo dynamics, before being applied to the actuator.

Boost – Air Temperature / RPM Compensation

Controls how desired boost pressure is altered depending on current atmospheric pressure.

EGT Limit

This map specifies the exhaust gas temperature at which a check engine light is illuminated. Of course an EGT sensor must be fitted – generally speaking, cars with up-pipe catalytic converters will already have this sensor.

VVT – Intake Cam Advance Angle

Specifies the intake cam advance, based on engine RPM and load. Careful dyno testing and data logging is required for effective alteration of this map. Timing changes will affect turbo spool up, peak torque and power. This map should only be enabled on cars that have VVT !!!

8.13 2D Maps

Duty Cycle / Atmospheric Pressure Compensation

Controls how the duty cycle is scaled, according to the current atmospheric pressure. E.g. At high atmospheric pressures, it is easier for the turbo to build boost, since the air it is compressing is denser. This means that a lower duty cycle is required at sea level for example, when compared with higher altitudes, in order to achieve the same boost pressure.

Duty Cycle / Air Intake Temperature Compensation

Controls how the duty cycle is scaled according to the current air temperature, as measured at the air intake of the car. At low temperatures, air is denser, meaning that a lower duty cycle is required in order to produce a given level of boost.

Duty Cycle / Coolant Temperature Compensation

Controls how the duty cycle is scaled according to the current coolant temperature of the engine. This may be used to protect the engine from damage at very high/low temperatures by dropping the boost away.

Boost Pressure / Coolant Temperature Compensation

Controls how the desired boost pressure is scaled according to the current coolant temperature of the engine. This may be used to protect the engine from damage at very high/low temperatures by dropping the boost away.

Boost Achieve / Atmospheric Pressure Compensation

Controls how desired boost pressure is scaled depending on the current atmospheric pressure.

Boost Limit

Determines the boost limit based on current atmospheric pressure. This is necessary since all boost pressure values are absolute, not atmospheric relative. When altering this map, ensure that all values are altered i.e. to add 0.1bar to the boost limit, add 0.1bar to all values in the map. If the boost limiting is triggered, fuel cut will occur to protect the engine. Boost limiting is triggered when the boost pressure exceeds the boost limit for a short period. To prevent fuel cut, the boost pressure must quickly drop below the boost limit. This effectively allows a brief spike to occur without fuel cut, with fuel cut occurring if this high level is sustained. Because of this, the boost limit set must be at least 0.1 bar above the maximum sustained boost pressure to prevent fuel cut.

Boost Solenoid Warning MAP Threshold

This map determines the absolute manifold pressure at which the turbocharger waste gate solenoid warning light is triggered. If the boost limit is raised, the values in this map should be increased accordingly.

Air Flow Sensor Scaling

Determines how airflow sensor voltage is converted into an airflow rate value. This map may be modified if the car is fitted with an induction kit that alters airflow, or a non-standard air flow meter. To correctly achieve this, requires flow testing and measurement of the new devices.

Turbo Dynamics

These maps control the rate at which the waste gate duty cycle is altered in order to produce the desired level of boost. These maps determine the percentage of waste gate duty that is added or subtracted from the current duty, based on the magnitude of error between actual boost and desired boost. Small values in these maps will cause the boost to build very slowly, but are very safe, since there will be no over boost. Higher values in these maps will causes boost to rise more aggressively, but must be carefully set to ensure that over boost and oscillation do not occur.

Proportional Burst

Initial values of compensation are taken from this map to give a burst of duty when stamping on the throttle for example.

Proportional Continuous

Subsequent compensation values are taken from this map. Values in the continuous map tend to be smaller than in the burst map.

Integral Positive & Negative

Some newer ECUs also have integral compensation for boost error. These maps add or subtract duty from the current duty, according to on how long the boost error has persisted for, as well as how large the error is. The values in these maps are small, but help to maintain faster responding control of boost. There may be two integral maps, split into positive and negative regions. One is used when boost is too high (the negative compensation map), the other is used when boost is too low (the positive compensation map).

Injector Battery Voltage Compensation

This map controls the injector opening time compensation for battery voltage. Each injector type has different mechanical characteristics, and the time that the injector takes to open before any fuel flows is based on the exact car battery voltage. This map allows the compensation to be matched to any injectors that are used on the car.

Ignition Timing Intake Air Temperature Compensation

Allows the ignition timing to be altered based on air temperature.

MAF Sensor Flow Limit Warning

Specifies the airflow rate at which the warning light is illuminated.

Open/Closed Loop Fuelling Throttle Threshold

Specifies the throttle position (according to engine RPM) at which the ECU switches from closed loop to open loop fuelling. Can be very useful on turbo cars to prevent the engine from running high boost at stoichiometric fuel mixtures due to exhaust & induction upgrades.

8.14 1D Maps - Data Values

Rev Limit

Two stage engine rev limit. The first value is the RPM at which the rev limit begins. The second value is the RPM at which the rev limiting switches off again. It is advised that these two numbers are set at least 200rpm apart so that the engine speed must drop by 200RPM before the rev limit switches off.

Rev Limit Ignition Retard

When rev limiting, some ECUs allow additional ignition retard to be applied. This parameter specifies this retard value.

Fuel Map Knock Switch Threshold

The advance multiplier threshold at which the ECU applies knock correction. The value ranges from 0 to 15, 0 being bad, 15 being good. If the advance multiplier drops below the knock switch threshold, then the knock map will be referenced. The advance multiplier may be considered as a long term knock correction indicator – high values indicate that the ECU is willing to use large values of ignition advance. Low values indicate the ECU is not willing to advance timing.

Knock Learning Thresholds

Some ECUs continuously maintains a table of learnt knock correction. The table is usually 8x8 in size, with 8 columns for engine load, and 8 rows for RPM ranges. It is possible to alter the dividers between these zones in order to spread the learnt correction across a wider range of loads or RPMs. E.g.. when boost levels are raised, the engine will achieve higher loads that were previously possible. In these circumstances, the knock learning load zones may be spread across the new (larger) range of load values.

Boost Based Speed Limiting

Allows a very soft limiting of vehicle speed by controlling boost pressure – the boost pressure gradually drops away to spring tension as the upper limit is approached. This feature is very useful, but is set very high on default ECU maps. Many independent tests have shown that top mount intercoolers receives little air flow at high vehicle speeds and charge temperatures rise rapidly – just watch the knock correction as the car is driven hard in 4th & 5th gear for confirmation. This feature may be used to restrict boost pressure at very high speeds, and could save an engine from damage.

Intercooler Auto-Wash Thresholds

For vehicles fitted with automatic intercooler water spray, these thresholds for coolant temperature, RPM, boost pressure, vehicle speed & air temperature control when the water spray is switched on. All of the criteria must be met for the spray to be enabled. Each parameter, such as RPM, has two threshold values. The first value is the point at which the spray turns on, whilst the second value is point at which the spray turns off.

Per Gear Boost Control

These maps allow adjustment of boost parameters for each gear. These values apply to manual transmission cars only. Most ECUs do not have this feature, whilst some ECUs only have one of the two maps below.

Per Gear Boost Compensation

This map allows the desired boost for each gear to be adjusted.

Per Gear Waste gate Duty Compensation

This map allows the waste gate duty to be adjusted for each gear. For example, lower gears require a higher waste gate duty in order to produce the same level of boost. This map could be used to address this.

Gear Compensation Disable Speed

This is the vehicle speed at which per gear compensation is switched off. This may need altering before the above maps will take effect.

Speed Limiting

This map allows adjustment of vehicle speed limiting. There are 2 values associated with speed limiting. One value is the speed at which limiting begins. The second value is the speed to which the vehicle must drop before speed limiting ends.

9. Getting Started

9.1 Overview of EMU Manufacturers

This section gives a list of the most popular EMUs on the market.

MoTeC
MoTeC is an Australian company. Been producing ECUs since 1987.
Worked closely with major racing, rally teams, competition engine companies and automobile manufacturers.
ECUs, Data Acquisition, Overrun Boost Enhancement and Boost Control on rally cars, Traction Control, Full Throttle Upshifts and Gear Dependant Shift Lights on race cars, Close Loop Lambda Control (Narrow Band & Wide Band), Idle Speed Control and Sophisticated Acceleration/Deceleration Enrichment/Enleanment on road cars.

Gems - General Engine Management Systems
GEMS have been designing and producing electronic systems for the automotive and motorsport industries since the early 1980's, providing systems to all levels including top factory teams such as Subaru and Peugeot. They provide:
*   Engine Management Systems – Flexible, reliable and cost-effective EMS solutions.
*   Active Systems – Powerful active control systems.
*   Data Acquisition Systems – Fully configurable, powerful data acquisition systems.
*   Display Systems – Fully configurable in-car display systems for driver, co-driver and engineer.
AEM and Omex are repackaged GEMS ECUs

Pectel
Pectel Control Systems is based in the UK, they are an established company which has specialized in the supply of automotive electronic systems for more than ten years.
They have built up successful partnerships with a number of leading manufacturers and motorsport teams, many of whom have enjoyed considerable success.

Autronic
Autronic is a Australian owned company that is based in Melbourne. The company was formed in 1987. Autronic now produces three engine management models, the SMC,SM2 and SM4 plus replacement boards for Subaru WRX and Mitsubishi EVO cars. All offer three dimensional mapping of fuel and ignition and are full sequential. Also two exhaust gas analysers, the A and B models.

Bosch Motorsport
Bosch Motorsport work on comprehensive motor racing systems. Supply ECUs to teams from the DTM and Formula 3 and to Skoda World Rally Championship team.

Magneti Marelli
Higher level applications where complete integration of data acquisition and chassis control is required within one package.

DTA Fast
These are intended for use in competition vehicles but they also have applications in high performance modified road vehicles.

Emerald
Based in Watton, Norfolk (close to Snetterton circuit and Lotus HQ in Hethel). Sell the M3DK engine management system. The M3DK handles full 3D mapping of both ignition and injection on most normally aspirated and turbo engines. Emerald produced the first M3D management system in 1994 as ignition only and soon after fuel injection was added. They now have a 32-bit system using Windows control.

Link Engine Management

The LEM is a very flexible, powerful engine management system. It is configurable to suit about 70% of the automotive engines available today. MiataLink 1.6 for MX5.

HKS Systems

The HKS F-CON range are a plug-in engine management system that provides full fuel management tuning and ignition timing control capability by utilizing the factory fuel and ignition baseline curves as reference points to configure a new fuel & ignition maps.

Apexi Systems

A'PEX Co. Ltd. was founded in 1992. Multinational firm with over 230 employees boasting: a suspension manufacturing plant, an exhaust system manufacturing plant, a race car engineering centre.
All their electronic products are manufactured by third parties and resold.

9.2 Best ECUs for Different Marques

Toyota Celica GT4 ST165 to ST205
*   Motec M4 ECUs work very well with the GT4. The ST185 rally cars were developed in conjunction with the Motec M4/M48 and M8 ECUs. Direct plug in versions were produced in the 1990s to comply with gpN and gpA regulations.
*   The newer M400 and M800 also work very well on the ST205.
*   Apexi PowerFC is also very successful on all 3S-GT and GTE engines incl the MR2 from 1992 onwards. A special version of the PowerFC is available for the ST205 to control the water to air intercooler (the Motec M4 simply wires the cooler relay directly).
*   HKS Fcon Pro also works well with the GT4.
*   Piggyback ECUs that suit the GT4 are Unichip and Apexi SAFR Fuel Computer.

Gems also build an ECU specifically for the gpA GT4:
*   AEM Toyota Celica 1990-92
*   AEM Toyota Celica 1993
*   AEM Toyota MR2 1991-92 Turbo
*   AEM Toyota MR2 1993-95 Turbo

Toyota Corolla and Celica T-sport
*   Apexi Power FC,
*   HKS Fcon range,
*   Apexi SAFR

Toyota Supra MkIV
*   HKS Fcon piggyback
*   Motec M600/M800 ECU in piggyback
*   AEM Toyota Supra 1993-98 Twin Turbo 30-1100
*   AEM Toyota Supra 1987-88 Turbo 30-1110
*   AEM Toyota Supra 1993-98 N/A

Mitsubishi Evo 1 to 3
*   Motec M4/M48/M8
*   Motec M48 OEMECU
*   Gems Evo1/6 OEMECU

Mitsubishi Evo 4 to 8
*   Motec M400/M600/M800
*   Motec M800 OEMECU
*   Gems Evo 7/8 OEMECU
*   AEM Mitsubishi Lancer 2003 EVO VIII(Gems)

Mitsubishi Evo 9 to 10
*   Motec M400/M600/M800 with Cam Control
*   Motec M800 OEMECU with Cam Control

Subaru Impreza v1 to v4
- Motec M4/M48/M8
- Motec M48 OEMECU
- Gems Subaru 96 to 97
- Gems Subaru OEM 93-96(4 plug)
- Gems Subaru OEM 97(3 plug)

Subaru Impreza v5 to v10
- Motec M400/M600/M800
- Motec M800 OEMECU
- Gems Subaru 99
- Gems Subaru 2000 onwards Std
- Gems Subaru 2000 onwards with Logging
- Gems Subaru 99-00(3 grey plug)
- Gems Subaru 01-05(5 white plug)

Subaru Impreza v11 onwards
- Motec M400/M600/M800 with Cam Control
- Motec M800 OEMECU with Cam Control
- Gems Subaru 01-05(5 white plug) Cam Control

Nissan Skyline GTS/GTR
- Motec M800/M880 with I/O Extension
- Motec M600/M800 in piggyback
- Apexi PowerFC GTR
- HKS FconV Pro in piggyback
- Mines/Nismo EEPROM ECUs
- AEM Nissan Skyline 89-94 RB20DET M/T(Gems)
- AEM Nissan Skyline 99-03 RB26DETT M/T(Gems)
- AEM Nissan Skyline 89-98 RD26DETT M/T(Gems)
- AEM Nissan Skyline 93-98 RB25DET M/T(Gems)

S13 180SX/S14 200SX/S15 Sylvia
- HKS Fcon Pro
- Apexi PowerFC
- AEM PnP Series of ECUs

300ZX
- Motec/AEM and PowerFC

Mazda MX5
- Link Maita PlugIn
- AEM Miata

RX7
- Apexi PowerFC
- AEM RX-7 1993-95

Honda B16/B18 engines 1992 to 2000
- Apexi PowerFC
- Motec for rallying
- Apexi SAFR Fuel Computer
- Unichip Piggyback ECU

K20 engines 2001 to present
- Apexi PowerFC
- Motec M400
- Hondata Kpro

Ford Escort Cosworth
- Pectel S4
- Motec M48

Escort MkI and Mk2 EFI
- Millington/BDA – Any

Ford Puma gpA
- Pectel E4 Only

Ford Ka gpA
- Motec M4 Pro Only

9.3 Most Popular ECU Reprogramming Software

MoTeC M4/M48/M8 DOS Based Software

- DOS based software.
- Very intuitive – excellent graphing function.
- Most modern graphing functionality is still not as good.
- Requires some time to familiarise yourself with the many functions available.
- Very few functions are automated which makes the ECUs very configurable but also makes them more complicated.
- No knock detection.

MoTeC M400/600/800 Windows Software

- Follow on from the DOS based software.
- Controls all new generation MoTeC ECUs.
- Common look and feel across the whole MoTeC range of products including the Data logging and telemetry software. This saves time when switching from the ECU to the logging software.
- No knock detection.

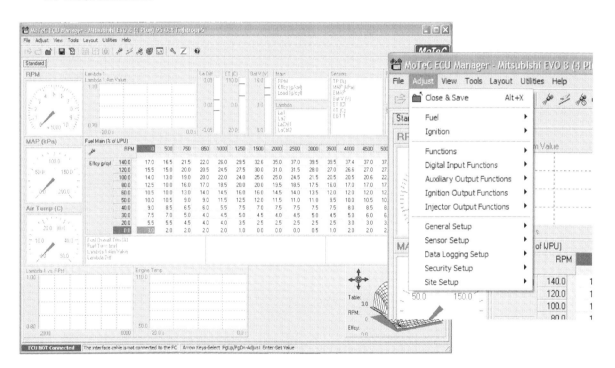

GEMS ECU Software

- Windows based.
- Software forms the basis of all of the Gems family of ECUs including the OMEX and AEM products.
- Simple menu layout but can get messy.
- The Menu system is fully user configurable, but in default mode, all the compensation tables are bunched into a single menu and simply sorted alphabetically.
- This can make the final setup of the ECU much more time consuming.
- Most rally mappers tend to simply copy the MoTeC template and transfer it over to the Gems software.
- No knock detection.

HKS Fcon Software
- Takes a lot of the functionality and places it into parameter windows.
- This simplifies the initial setup for each new vehicle.
- Fuel and ignition tables are unnecessarily detailed which can slow down the mapping process and thus place additional demands on the vehicle.
- Only superficial graphing facility available.
- No knock detection.

Hondata K-Series Software
- Designed specifically for variable CAM (Honda) vehicles.
- A unique method for mapping variable CAM parameters.
- There are six individual fuel and ignition tables, along with two CAM tables.
- No real 3D graphing capability.
- Very unreliable upload and download capability. This means that uploading and downloading outside of the dyno environment can be hit and miss.
- Good knock detection algorithms.

Autronic Software
- Autronic software is an attempt to provide all the MoTeC functionality without the associated complexity.
- Can initially appear messy and a bit amateurish, but tends to work well on mainstream vehicles such as Evos and Subarus.
- Can be difficult to implement on odd-ball projects like GTRs.
- Graphing function is excellent.
- No knock detection.

OMEX Software
(Same as Gems)

Greddy Emanage Piggyback Software
- Good stab at bringing mainstream software functionality to the piggyback user.
- Simple operation and reliable upload and download.
- Far superior to Unichip software.

9.4 Checklist for ECU (or EMU) Setup

This section gives the reader a practical checklist for setting up an ECU from scratch. Most ECUs are very similar in design. For this section I've decided to use the Motec M800 ECU as an example.

9.4.1 ECU Functions

The most basic functions available on any ECU are:
- Basic Fuel Control
- Basic Ignition Control
- Basic Boost Control
- All major engine actuator control.
- All major engine sensor reading.

Additional features of ECU may include:
- Data Logging. Allows logging of the ECU sensors and operating parameters to the internal data logging memory. The logged data may then be analysed.
- Wideband Lambda. Allows Wideband Lambda (Air Fuel Ratio) measurement, which may be used for data logging or closed loop control of the Air Fuel Ratio. Bosch LSU or NTK wideband lambda sensors are the norm.
- Telemetry. Enables the ECU to send telemetry data via a radio to the pits.

Other features may include:
- CAM Control
- Drive by Wire
- Traction Control
- Overrun Boost Enhancement
- Gear Change Ignition Cut
- Hi/Lo Injection
- Servo Motor Control
- Multi-pulse Injection

9.4.2 ECU Inputs & Outputs

The ECU analyses signals from the sensors, then controls the Fuel Injectors, Ignition System and other auxiliary devices according to the Calibration and Setup Data which is stored in the ECUs programmable memory. The Inputs and Outputs are shown on the right:

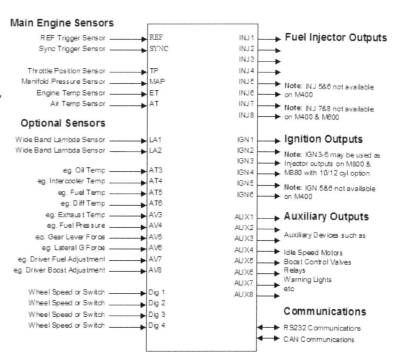

Main Engine Sensors

The Main Engine Sensors are required for correct operation of the ECU.
- The engine RPM is derived from the REF trigger sensor.
- The SYNC trigger sensor is required to synchronize the Fuel and Ignition to the correct engine cycle for sequential injection and correct firing of multicoil ignition systems.
- The Throttle Position, Manifold Pressure, Air Temp and Engine Temp are used as inputs to the various calibration tables.

Optional Sensors

The Optional Sensors are not required for basic operation of the ECU.
- The Lambda Inputs may be used for wideband air fuel ratio measurement or wideband or narrow band closed loop lambda control.
- The Digital Inputs may be used for wheel speed measurement or to activate functions such as Dual RPM Limit, or Nitrous.
- The other inputs may be used for data logging (e.g.. Exhaust Gas Temp, Gear Box Temp, Driver Boost adjustment etc.) or for special calibration features.

Fuel Injector Outputs

- Up to twelve injectors may be driven fully sequentially by the ECU if the injectors are high resistance types (12 ohms or greater), otherwise up to eight injectors may be driven fully sequentially including very low ohm types (0.5 ohms).
- Four of the Ignition Outputs are used for full sequential 12 cylinder operation.
- Twelve cylinder engines may also be driven as six groups of 2 injectors which leaves all six Ignition outputs available for wasted spark ignition.
- Outputs not used for Fuel Injection may be used as Auxiliary Outputs.

Ignition Outputs

The Ignition Outputs may be used to drive many different types of ignition systems, which are detailed in the various ignition system drawings.

Auxiliary Outputs

The ECU's have eight Auxiliary Outputs that may be used for :
Turbo Waste Gate Control, CAM Control, Idle Speed Control, Gear Change Light, Driver Warning Alarm (plus many others).

6.4.3 Calibration and Setup

Calibration Tables

The Calibration Tables determine how the output devices should be controlled for various sensor readings. For example the fuel calibration table determines the base injector pulse width for all combinations of RPM and Load. Other calibration tables will also affect the fuel injector pulse width such as Air Temperature compensation and Engine Temperature compensation.

The ECU determines the amount of fuel to inject by first calculating the RPM and Load then extracting the corresponding value from the table. If the RPM and Load do not match an RPM and LOAD point exactly then the values from the closest sites are mathematically interpolated to arrive at an intermediate value.

Setup Parameters

The Setup Parameters allow the ECU to be configured for almost any engine. The Setup Parameters include Number of Cylinders, Ignition Type, Sensor Types, Injector Current, Auxiliary Output Functions etc..

9.4.4 Main Setup

Injectors
- Injector Scaling (IJPU)
- Injector Current
- Injector Battery Compensation

Calculation Methods
- Efficiency Calculation Method.
- Load Calculation Method.

Load Sites Selection
Selects the range of load points to suit the selected sensors operational range.

Number of Cylinders
- 4 Stroke engines : use positive numbers e.g.. 8 for 8 cyl.
- 2 Stroke engines : use negative numbers e.g.. -2 for 2 cyl.
- Rotary engines : use -2 for 2 rotor and -3 for 3 rotor.

Trigger Setup
- Ref / Sync Mode (REF)
- Crank Reference Teeth (CRT)
- Crank Index Position (CRIP)

Ignition
- Ignition Type (IGN)
- Number of Coils (COIL)
- Ignition Dwell Time (DELL)
- Ignition Delay Time

9.4.5 Sensor Setup

Throttle Position Sensor Hi / Lo
TPLO   Throttle Position LO (Closed Throttle)
TPHI   Throttle Position HI (Wide Open Throttle)
The Throttle HI and LO points must be set every time the throttle position sensor is moved or replaced so that the throttle can be correctly scaled between 0 and 100%.

REF/SYNC Sensor Setup
The REF/SYNC setup parameters must be set to suit the trigger sensors.

Sensor Calibrations
The sensors calibrations must be set to suit the connected sensors.

9.4.6 Fuel and Ignition Tables (Initial Calibration)

Fuel - Main Table
- Check the Fuel - Main Table.
- The table should be smooth. In general turbo tables look quite different from throttle position tables, so it is wise to start with a table from a similar engine.

Fuel - Air Temp
Check the Fuel - Air Temp compensation table.

Fuel - Engine Temp
The Fuel - Engine Temp compensation table may be used instead of the cold start warm up parameter.

Fuel - MAP
Check the Fuel - MAP compensation table.
The fuel must be increased by 100% every 100 kPa increase in air pressure.

Normally the MAP table should contain the following values, with a straight line increase between values.
(MOTEC TABLE)

0 kPa	100 kPa	200 kPa	300 kPa	400 kPa	500 kPa
-100	0	100	200	300	400

This table is equally applicable whether the MAP sensor is used for barometric pressure measurement or for manifold pressure measurement.
Note that the higher pressure sites will only be available if a high pressure MAP sensor is used.

Fuel - Cold Start
- Fuel - Acceleration Enrichment
- Generally acceleration enrichment is not required above 4000 RPM.

Typically all other fuel compensation tables should bet set to zero for initial calibration.

Ignition - Main Table
The table should be smooth.
Make sure that the Ignition - Main Table is initialized with a conservative curve for the particular engine, not too advanced and not too retarded.

Ignition - Air Temp
Check the Ignition - Air Temp compensation table.

Typically all other ignition compensation tables should bet set to zero for initial calibration.

9.4.7 Pre Start Checks

Calibration Tables & Setup Parameters

Check that all Setup Parameters have been set appropriately.
Check that all calibration tables have sensible values in them.
Check that any advanced functions such as Traction Control are turned off.

Power to the ECU

If the ECU has power then the software should indicate that the ECU is connected

Diagnostic Errors

Before starting the engine check the diagnostics errors. Any errors must be rectified before starting the Engine.

Sensor Errors

If an error is shown for a sensor that is not fitted the sensor should be disabled by setting the sensor setup number to zero. Sensor Errors may be due to bad wiring to the Sensor (either short circuit or open circuit).

Test the Sensors

Before starting the engine test that all sensors are giving sensible readings by viewing their values . Vary the sensor readings if possible to check for correct operation.
Check that the Throttle Position Sensor varies smoothly from 0 to 100% when moved from fully closed to fully open.
The MAP sensor should read barometric pressure when the engine is stopped (approximately 100 to 102 kPa at sea level depending on the day).
The Engine Temp and Air Temp sensors must give correct readings.

Test the Ignition

Use the Ignition Test to ensure that the Ignition System is functioning correctly.
Some special ignition systems do not work in the Ignition Test screen. e.g.. Mazda Series 4 & 5 and other direct fire ignition systems. If the Ignition System is wired via the Fuel Pump relay then the ignition test will not work unless this relay is activated. It will be necessary to place a spark plug on the lead from the ignition coil if the ignition system uses a distributor.

Test the Injectors

Use the software to ensure that all injectors are working and that they are wired in the correct firing order for sequential operation.
WARNING: Ensure that the fuel pump is off during this test.

Initial Cranking

- Crank the engine without fuel pressure and check the RPM reading.
- Check that the RPM reading is sensible, if the RPM is too high or too low or is erratic then the Setup may be incorrect or there may be a problem with the REF sensor signal. If there is no RPM reading then the REF sensor is not working.
- Check that no REF or SYNC Diagnostic Errors occur during constant cranking. Diagnostic errors may occur as cranking winds up, this is OK, but the errors need to be cleared so that constant cranking may be checked for errors. Diagnostic errors may occur as cranking winds down, this is also OK.

Cranking Ignition Timing

Check that the Ignition Timing is correct during constant cranking.

9.4.8 Starting

Fuel System
Power up the fuel pumps and check the fuel system for leaks before attempting to start the engine.

Fuel Overall Trim
Use the Trim to vary the mixture when trying to start the engine to see if the engine needs more or less fuel, this ensures that the mixture is varied equally for all RPM and Load points.
Establish how much trim the engine needs on average then trim the tables directly.

If the Engine won't start
- Check for correct fuel pressure.
- Check for fouled plugs.
- Re-check for diagnostics errors.
- Re-check the Ignition Timing with a Timing Light.
- Check the setup parameters against the drawings.
- Check that the ignition is wired in the correct firing order.
- Check that the ignition is firing on the compression stroke, not the exhaust stroke.

After Start Checks:

Ignition Timing Check
Check the Ignition Timing with a Timing Light to ensure that the actual Ignition Timing corresponds to the ECU Ignition Timing.

Fuel Pressure
Check that correct fuel pressure is maintained under all load conditions.

9.4.9 Diagnostic Errors (Operational)

After the engine has started check for diagnostics errors.
The following operational errors may occur in a new installation.

Injector Errors

Open   The Injector is open circuit - check the wiring.
Short   The Injector is short circuit - check the wiring.
Peak   The Injector peak current was not reached.
Possible causes :
* The Injector Current Setup Parameter IJCU is set too high.
* The battery voltage is too low.

Over Duty Error

The injector duty cycle is too high, typically the duty cycle should not exceed 85%.
If the injectors exceed their maximum duty then larger injectors or higher fuel pressure is needed.

REF / SYNC Errors

The possible causes of the various errors are detailed below :

REF Error

Too many REF pulses have occurred between SYNC pulses.
Possible causes :
* A bad REF signal has caused extra pulses or a SYNC pulse has been missed - check voltage levels with a scope.
* Bad REF / SYNC alignment.
* Incorrect Setup

No REF Error

Two SYNC signals have occurred without a REF signal.
Possible causes :
* If the RPM is 0 then there is no signal - check the wiring and sensor voltage levels with a scope.
* If RPM is not 0 then a bad SYNC signal has caused extra pulses - check voltage levels with a scope.
* If RPM is low then the REF and SYNC signals may have been swapped.
* Incorrect Setup

SYNC Error

The SYNC signal has occurred before expected.
Possible causes :
* A bad SYNC signal has caused extra SYNC pulses - check voltage levels with a scope.
* A bad REF signal has caused missing REF pulses - check voltage levels with a scope.
* Bad REF / SYNC alignment.
* Incorrect Setup

No SYNC Error

Two or more consecutive SYNC pulses are missing.
Possible causes :
* No SYNC signal - check the wiring and SYNC sensor voltage levels with a scope.
* A bad REF signal has caused many extra pulses - check voltage levels with a scope.
* Incorrect Setup

Multiple REF / SYNC Errors

Multiple REF / SYNC errors may occur, often the first error to occur is the correct error.
Multiple errors may also occur due to incorrect Setup.

9.4.10 Dyno Calibration

- The alternator should be connected while tuning the engine to ensure that the injectors are working at normal operating voltage.
- The exhaust system should be the same as that in the vehicle as it will effect the engine tuning.
- On multi runner intake manifolds the air box should be fitted as it is an integral part of the intake system and will effect the engine tuning.
- The fuel pressure is critical to the injector flow and should be monitored during dyno tuning. Incorrect fuel pressure will result in incorrect tuning. Note that on turbo engines the fuel pressure will vary as the manifold pressure varies because the regulator maintains a fixed pressure above manifold pressure.

9.4.11 Main Table Calibrations

Fuel - Main Table
Allows adjustment of the fuel at various RPM and Load points.
Work through all the table values systematically so that all points are adjusted for the correct Air Fuel Ratio reading.
Use extreme caution when adjusting the fuel to ensure that the engine does not run lean at high loads. It is best to start rich. A temperature compensated wide band Air Fuel Ratio Meter is essential to ensure correct air fuel ratio.

If the engine is missing for any reason (including over rich) the sensor may falsely read lean due to the oxygen in the un-burnt mixture.
The Air Fuel Ratio should be adjusted according to the engine load and the desired results, for example power, economy, emissions etc.. At high loads the mixture should be approximately 0.89 Lambda for maximum power. On turbo charged engines a richer mixture may be required to reduce exhaust temperatures and help avoid knocking. At lighter loads the mixture may be adjusted for best emissions (1.00 Lambda) or best economy (1.05 Lambda).

The cranking (starting) fuel may be adjusted by adjusting the 0 RPM load sites. Typically more fuel is required at cranking than at idle RPM.

Ignition - Main Table
Allows adjustment of the Ignition Timing at various RPM and Load points.
Start with a conservative curve for the particular engine, not too advanced and not too retarded.
Use extreme caution when adjusting the Ignition Timing to ensure that the engine does not knock due to excessive advance. Re-check the Ignition Timing with a Timing Light to ensure that the what the ECU thinks is the ignition advance is in fact the actual advance.

The Ignition Timing should be adjusted for maximum torque without knocking, by increasing the advance until the torque stops increasing. Make sure there is at least 3 or 4 degrees margin to the knock limit.
Too much retard will cause excessive exhaust gas temperature.
At idle a more retarded ignition setting is desirable (approximately 10 to 15 degrees). This makes the idle speed less sensitive to load changes. Also the ignition should be flat over the idle RPM range so that timing variations do not cause the engine to hunt, since variations in the timing will vary the engine torque.

Fuel Cold Start
The Cold Start parameters may be adjusted after the Fuel - Main Table has been adjusted and the 0 RPM sites have been adjusted for good hot starting.

Appendix A

A1. Boost

Bar	PSI 14.50	kPa 100.00	inHg 29.92
0.10	1.45	10.00	2.99
0.20	2.90	20.00	5.98
0.30	4.35	30.00	8.98
0.40	5.80	40.00	11.97
0.50	7.25	50.00	14.96
0.60	8.70	60.00	17.95
0.70	10.15	70.00	20.94
0.80	11.60	80.00	23.94
0.90	13.05	90.00	26.93
1.00	14.50	100.00	29.92
1.10	15.95	110.00	32.91
1.20	17.40	120.00	35.90
1.30	18.85	130.00	38.90
1.40	20.31	140.00	41.89
1.50	21.76	150.00	44.88
1.60	23.21	160.00	47.87
1.70	24.66	170.00	50.86
1.80	26.11	180.00	53.86
1.90	27.56	190.00	56.85
2.00	29.01	200.00	59.84
2.10	30.46	210.00	62.83
2.20	31.91	220.00	65.82
2.30	33.36	230.00	68.82
2.40	34.81	240.00	71.81
2.50	36.26	250.00	74.80
2.60	37.71	260.00	77.79
2.70	39.16	270.00	80.78
2.80	40.61	280.00	83.78
2.90	42.06	290.00	86.77
3.00	43.51	300.00	89.76

A2. Lambda

Lambda			

Lam	AFR 14.70	Lam	AFR
0.50	7.35	0.75	11.03
0.55	8.09	0.76	11.17
0.60	8.82	0.77	11.32
0.65	9.56	0.78	11.47
0.70	10.29	0.79	11.61
0.75	11.03	0.80	11.76
0.80	11.76	0.81	11.91
0.85	12.50	0.82	12.05
0.90	13.23	0.83	12.20
0.95	13.97	0.84	12.35
1.00	14.70	0.85	12.50
1.05	15.44	0.86	12.64
1.10	16.17	0.87	12.79
1.15	16.91	0.88	12.94
1.20	17.64	0.89	13.08
1.25	18.38	0.90	13.23
1.30	19.11	0.91	13.38
1.35	19.85	0.92	13.52
1.40	20.58	0.93	13.67
1.45	21.32	0.94	13.82
1.50	22.05	0.95	13.97
1.55	22.79	0.96	14.11
1.60	23.52	0.97	14.26
1.65	24.26	0.98	14.41
1.70	24.99	0.99	14.55
1.75	25.73	1.00	14.70
1.80	26.46	1.01	14.85
1.85	27.20	1.02	14.99
1.90	27.93	1.03	15.14
1.95	28.67	1.04	15.29

A3. Torque

Torque			
FtLb	Nm 1.36	**FtLb**	Nm
10	13.56	310	420.30
20	27.12	320	433.86
30	40.67	330	447.42
40	54.23	340	460.98
50	67.79	350	474.54
60	81.35	360	488.09
70	94.91	370	501.65
80	108.47	380	515.21
90	122.02	390	528.77
100	135.58	400	542.33
110	149.14	410	555.89
120	162.70	420	569.44
130	176.26	430	583.00
140	189.81	440	596.56
150	203.37	450	610.12
160	216.93	460	623.68
170	230.49	470	637.23
180	244.05	480	650.79
190	257.61	490	664.35
200	271.16	500	677.91
210	284.72	510	691.47
220	298.28	520	705.03
230	311.84	530	718.58
240	325.40	540	732.14
250	338.95	550	745.70
260	352.51	560	759.26
270	366.07	570	772.82
280	379.63	580	786.37
290	393.19	590	799.93
300	406.75	600	813.49

A4. BHP

Power

BHP	PS	kW	BHP	PS	kW
	1.00	0.75			
10	10.00	7.46	310	310.00	231.17
20	20.00	14.91	320	320.00	238.62
30	30.00	22.37	330	330.00	246.08
40	40.00	29.83	340	340.00	253.54
50	50.00	37.29	350	350.00	261.00
60	60.00	44.74	360	360.00	268.45
70	70.00	52.20	370	370.00	275.91
80	80.00	59.66	380	380.00	283.37
90	90.00	67.11	390	390.00	290.82
100	100.00	74.57	400	400.00	298.28
110	110.00	82.03	410	410.00	305.74
120	120.00	89.48	420	420.00	313.19
130	130.00	96.94	430	430.00	320.65
140	140.00	104.40	440	440.00	328.11
150	150.00	111.86	450	450.00	335.57
160	160.00	119.31	460	460.00	343.02
170	170.00	126.77	470	470.00	350.48
180	180.00	134.23	480	480.00	357.94
190	190.00	141.68	490	490.00	365.39
200	200.00	149.14	500	500.00	372.85
210	210.00	156.60	510	510.00	380.31
220	220.00	164.05	520	520.00	387.76
230	230.00	171.51	530	530.00	395.22
240	240.00	178.97	540	540.00	402.68
250	250.00	186.43	550	550.00	410.14
260	260.00	193.88	560	560.00	417.59
270	270.00	201.34	570	570.00	425.05
280	280.00	208.80	580	580.00	432.51
290	290.00	216.25	590	590.00	439.96
300	300.00	223.71	600	600.00	447.42

Printed in Great Britain
by Amazon.co.uk, Ltd.,
Marston Gate.